High Heels and
Holiness

DISCARDED

Also by Jo Saxton

Influential: Women in Leadership at Church, Work and Beyond
Real God, Real Life: Finding a spirituality that works

High Heels and Holiness

The Smart Girl's Guide
to Living Life Well

JO SAXTON

with Sally Breen

HODDER

First published in Great Britain in 2012 by Hodder & Stoughton
An Hachette UK company

This paperback edition first published in 2013.

1

A CIP catalogue record for this title is available from the British Library

ISBN 978 0 340 99532 7
eBook ISBN 978 0 340 99531 0

Typeset in Adobe Garamond by Hewer Text UK Ltd, Edinburgh

Printed and bound in the UK by CPI Group (UK) Ltd, Croydon CR0 4YY

Hodder & Stoughton policy is to use papers that are natural, renewable
and recyclable products and made from wood grown in sustainable forests.
The logging and manufacturing processes are expected to conform
to the environmental regulations of the country of origin.

Hodder & Stoughton Ltd
338 Euston Road
London NW1 3BH

www.hodderfaith.com

Dedication

To my sister Catherine Oyeniran, beautiful inside and out! Sis, you're a wonderful encouragement and a great role model. You're fab, you are.

– Jo

For Rebecca and Elizabeth. You each continue to open up places in my heart and I am so very proud of you both. And for my new daughter-in-law Taylor: I couldn't ask for a better wife or friend for Sam.

– Sally

Contents

Thank you!

To my girls Tia and Zoë: let's go play! To my love, Chris – thanks for the encouragement and unyielding support, and the late-night trips for snacks. Thanks to my 'book keepers' Zan, Bry and Lorn, and to Katherine Venn for being a great friend. To all the amazing women who've invited me to walk with them on their journey – it's been an honour to be with you. Special love for my huddle girls in Torrance: you've been an inspiration and a great support. But I will never camp in the wilderness with you again. And finally to Sal! Thanks for the love and the laughter, the food, your wisdom and your friendship – fifteen years and counting!

– Jo Saxton

First, thanks have to go to Jo, both for including me in the book and for allowing me to walk alongside her for the last fifteen years. It's been a privilege, a joy and a journey. Thanks to all the young women who have included me in their lives; I've loved spending time with you and getting to know each one of you. This book is for you; I hope you find it useful spiritually and practically. And Mike – thanks for always believing I had something to say.

– Sally Breen

Our love and thanks go to all the women who shared their stories and their hearts in the chapters of this book. You know who you are, and we're grateful for you. Finally, massive thanks to Team Hodder for all your hard work and perseverance with us on this project. Beyond the call of duty and deadline, yet again! With our love to you all.

Prologue

*Once upon a time, in a land far, far away, lived a beautiful princess.
Sadly, unbeknown to her, when she was just a young girl an evil spell
was cast over her. For years nothing happened. Yet as she grew into a
woman this spell gave her tormented dreams, night after night. There
was no escape. Her dreams followed the same pattern every night.*

*The princess was a beautiful woman and her beauty was expected to
last for ever. But in this dream, instead of being eternally young and
beautiful, the princess began to age. She discovered grey hairs, crow's
feet and lines across her face. Her metabolism, once bright and sprightly,
grew weary and began to slow down. The princess found that her body
shape began to change. She weighed more than she used to. Her body
no longer had the definition that it once did. Clothes were a little
tighter (or had they shrunk in the wash?). There was nothing she could
do to stop it.*

*In her world, the princess lived in a perfect castle, with exquisite
furnishings. Servants and handmaidens took care of her every need.
They listened to her every word, and lived to look after her. Yet in her
dream she lived in a tiny apartment with donated furniture and two
untidy women. One of the girls was always stealing the princess's food
because she spent all her money on clothes. The other girl was very*

beautiful and popular with all the guys. Not that our princess was jealous, because she was a princess after all, and besides, the other girl wasn't that beautiful.

In this terrible dream, the princess was not famous and known throughout the land for being – well, a princess. She had a job. And worse than that, it was a boring job, and did not fulfil her dreams or pay enough. Her boss was a pain and often took her for granted. She did not get the promotion she knew she deserved. She worked long hours and nobody recognised her for it: not even a thank you. The princess was not famous. In fact she was nobody special at all.

The princess was destined to marry a handsome prince, a gorgeous gallant warrior made for greatness. They would have a beautiful wedding, the best in all the kingdom. They would honeymoon in distant tropical lands. He would be perfect in every way and treat her as she deserved. They would live – yes – happily ever after.

But in her dream the man she met was an average guy (thankfully not a frog) with an average job. He did not have a warrior's physique but was ordinary, with emerging love handles. He was still trying to work out what to do with his life, so how was he ever going to come to her rescue?

The princess expected a perfect castle, filled with the joy and laughter of a growing family, the smiles of a tiny baby. She would have time to see friends and would retain her pre-baby body. Her husband would be called the luckiest man in the entire kingdom. But her dreaded dream foretold a much smaller home with crying babies, sleepless nights, no energy for friends, no waistline after children and a stressed-out husband who insisted he was more tired than she was. She wondered if she had the power to wake herself up.

When indeed the dream was over, the princess would wake in a cold sweat, terrified of making a single move. When she had calmed down, she got out of bed and began the day, only to find that her dream was actually . . . reality.

The princess thought she was destined for a life of promise, romance, beauty and happily ever afters. But her dream promised nothing extraordinary. It was average, often dull and a lot of hard work. Even worse, it didn't look as though anyone was about to rescue her any time soon.

1

Walk with me

Wouldn't it be great if twenty-first-century womanhood came with a manual?

It's a complex time to be a woman. There are some wonderful realities and some devastating tragedies about the female experience. In the same era, around the world women are taking hold of new opportunities and rising through the echelons of society to greater positions of influence and power, while millions of others are utterly powerless, trafficked for sexual exploitation. Globally, gender-based violence maims and kills more women aged 15–44 than cancer, malaria, traffic accidents and war. Tearfund note on their website that 'Global poverty has a woman's face', suggesting that 70 per cent of those around the world living in poverty are women. In the United Kingdom many women enjoy freedom and flexibility in their career choices and lifestyles that not even their mothers experienced. Yet at the same time many other women are oppressed and held captive in abusive relationships (in 2009–10, 73 per cent of the victims of domestic violence in the UK were women). While girls are outperforming boys at every level of education, for all their skills and qualifications women in general are paid significantly less than their male counterparts, a difference of up to 16 per cent in pay (the figure rises to 39 per cent if the work's part-time). Women are underrepresented on company boards in the UK, and only 12.5 per cent of directors in FSTE 100 companies are women – in fact, 21 per cent of FTSE 100 companies have all-male boards. Despite a record number of female MPs, they are still outnumbered four to one in parliament. In 2009 the NHS reported that one in five adult women experiences depression, anxiety or suicidal thoughts. It's no wonder theologian Carolyn Custis James concludes, 'The landscape for women in the twenty-first century is a polarized world of extremes that, to be honest, is confusing to women.'[1]

It's a complex time to be a woman. And yet here we are in the midst of the complexity, trying to work out how to live our lives and be the women we're meant to be.

Wouldn't it be good to have a manual?

It would be a thick encyclopaedic guide that would be miraculously light and fit into your handbag, or better still an app on your phone. And it would cover everything you needed to know to make it in life. Everything. It would lead you to the perfect job and career (with great pay) with the best colleagues ever. They'd be better than colleagues, they'd be family. Work wouldn't feel like work because you enjoyed it so much. It would show you how to meet Mr Right and have the perfect wedding, great sex and a fantastic marriage. It would show you how to have perfect, shiny, beautiful, talented and intelligent children. It would show you how to play that game called life. And win.

Then there are the things that we'd hope were so ingrained in our lives there would be no need for a manual. It would simply be a part of twenty-first-century-woman's DNA and life. The perfect metabolism with a body that sprang back to shape after every challenge, even childbirth. Culinary skills that always wowed your guests and occasionally yourself, yet didn't add a single pound. You would have glowing natural beauty without embellishment, gorgeous hair and a sense of style in fashion and home. The money to buy whatever you needed to make your life look and be beautiful. There would be family members who you always got on with, in-laws who adored you and approved of your every decision and friends who were faithful and always there. We might add that we'd love a sense of inner security and confidence that was unaffected by criticism and envy. We'd be so secure there would be no fears to face. No past to run from, no present to escape from, and we wouldn't be intimidated by the future . . . A relationship with God that never wavered, not even slightly. Great home, great family, great career and a great you!

Sadly, we wake up to a different kind of reality, don't we? A bit like waking up from the fairytale and finding out that this is it. Reality. We embark on adulthood, *on womanhood*, with hopes and dreams and expectations. Those expectations are not formed in isolation. The world around us constantly communicates with us – offers its own manuals, as it were – on who we are, what we're worth and who we should aspire to be. It speaks to us about beauty and sex, money, relationships and womanhood. Some messages appal us, others empower and inspire, while others simply leave us conflicted and confused. These messages have been with us for years, shaping and defining us. Some even go back as far as our childhood, in the sweet stories and movies that laced our imagination, inspiring longings about love, life and happily ever after. They were stories that spoke of being rescued from scary things by a knight in shining armour, a one true love. Stories that told us who we were. That though we might look ordinary, actually we were princesses. And we dressed up and played and enjoyed the dream. It's a wonderful game – for little girls to play. Yet in recent years it seems as if the game has grown up with us. It's as though princesses have made a comeback, now as adults. TV shows introduce us to beautiful heiresses (real or fictitious), for whom life seems like a dream away from our reality, but a compelling dream nonetheless.

Maybe the princesses never actually went away. Our chick lit books and films feed us a steady diet of women in need of rescue, who are transformed and brought to life by a twenty-first-century knight.

Perhaps it would be great to be a woman, especially if we knew exactly what to want and who to be and how to get it.

Even the messages our church culture communicates about womanhood can be confusing. A friend attending a Christian camp went to visit the children's work. It was high-energy, fun stuff. Yet she couldn't help but wonder why, when it came to biblical teaching, the theme for the boys was about them being warriors ready to do battle for God's kingdom, and yet for the girls it was simply about being God's princesses. It was a spiritualised version of the passive princess culture that is so widespread in society.

On one level it's great to address the messages of our culture and add a divine slant. Obviously God is a king and, technically speaking, as His daughters that might make princesses out of us. But when being God's child is infused with a 'pretty in pink' message that stops at passive beauty, surely we are missing something. Why weren't these young girls being taught about spiritual warfare as the boys were? The last time I looked, both men and women encounter spiritual warfare on a regular basis. What are we saying if our assumption is that the only battle young women face or need to be equipped for is knowing that we are attractive in His eyes? Such an assumption leaves generations of women ill-equipped for the battles and opportunities they will encounter in this life. We don't need to rescue the princess image within our culture. We need to know and live for the King. The kingdom of God is primarily about the King, not us. It's about God's rule and reign in our lives and about His people representing Him with love and power in our world. The princess image in our culture is great entertainment. But it's a woefully inadequate metaphor for our lives as Christian women in the twenty-first century. Our lives have joys and heartaches. Our lives are complex. Our lives have questions with uneasy answers. We walk with God, and sometimes wonder where He fits and how He speaks into our questions of life:

What can I do to make myself feel secure, really secure?

How do I get past my past?

How do I find and choose Mr Right? And what does it mean if I don't?

When is it a good time to have kids?

What am I supposed to do with my life?

How do I have a relationship with God in this phase of my life?

There are many, many more – about money, health, body, friendships, calling. And while we're not asking ourselves all these questions all the time, at some point they come up, because they're all a part of everyday life.

Q. What are the big questions that you're asking about your own life right now?

With the manual nowhere to be seen and questions and situations that stubbornly refuse to resolve, it's easy to feel stuck. It's easy to be paralysed by fear, confusion or indecision. It's equally easy to drift along in our lives, not engaging with the opportunities and challenges that are laid out for us in this wonderful gift called life. It would be great to have some input, some guidance – just a few signposts along the way. For many of us, the longing to have someone to walk through this stuff with is so profound it's like a constant dull ache. Maybe that's the biggest question of all, after 'What should I do?' Is there anyone out there who could walk with me through this?

I WISH I HAD A MENTOR

We're bombarded with advice and resources as Christians in our teen years, helping us to build our self-esteem, work out how to make good choices about boys, alcohol and friends, learning that, yes, God really does love us. Then later on in the settled-with-family stage, there are some wonderful resources out there on parenting, marriage advice, raising families. But what about the years in between those two phases of life? So much can take place in our twenties. We can enter this decade in our lives as a uni student in halls and leave them as a married mother of two. How did *that* happen? Or we enter it in a long-term relationship, planning on marriage and kids, and turn thirty single, with a career that seems to be taking off – but this was not exactly the life that we expected. These are significant years, and yet we're not always sure that we have the tools to make the right kinds of decision, the best decisions. How can we know, when we've not been there before? Wouldn't it be great to get some input on the choices that really matter? It's no wonder that the statement 'I wish I had someone to mentor me, to disciple me' seems to be a universal cry from young adult Christian women today.

'Mentor' might be a new word, but 'disciple' isn't. The word 'disciple', in Greek *mathetes*, means learner. In the time of Jesus a disciple was more than an academic student who learned biblical teaching. Disciples was people who not only gleaned information from their rabbi, but also sought to imitate their rabbi's life. They didn't just want to know what the rabbi knew, they wanted to live as the rabbi lived. A common blessing in Jesus' time was 'May you be covered in the dust of your rabbi', which demonstrates the understanding that disciples walked so closely to the person they were learning from that they would pick up his dust as they walked through the dusty streets. When Jesus made disciples, they learned from His teaching, but they also learned to imitate His life.

Discipleship today is about learning to become more like Jesus. It is not just knowing more about Him and believing in Him. If we are His disciples, we're also saying that we want to learn how to imitate His life on every level. We'll learn to imitate His values, His passions and His priorities, and so our lives will reflect His life. Jesus knew that humanity needed a tangible example to pattern our own lives after. And so as He leaves the earth He issues the call to all His disciples to continue His work – to make disciples. This pattern continued through the early churches of the New Testament; when Paul wrote to the struggling Corinthian church, he advised them to 'Follow my example, as I follow the example of Christ' (1 Cor. 11:1).

There is so much we can learn from another believer's life. We can be inspired from a distance by another woman's life and the way God uses her to do incredible things, but what does this look like close up? We've heard that we need to find our security in Christ, but wonder what that looks like in practice when we feel painfully insecure. We've heard that Christ gives us a new identity, but when will it change the way we feel when we look in the mirror? We know that God knows the plans He has for us, but we can't help but wonder what that looks like amid so many options. It could be helpful to have someone to learn from. That's where discipleship comes to life.

How do you find people to learn from, examples to follow? Well, as you walk through life, they tend to be the ones who are just a bit further along on the journey than you. They probably wouldn't call themselves expert hikers by any means. Yet because they've walked this road a little while longer, they're a little more familiar with the terrain, better prepared than you for some of the conditions ahead. They've got the experience and the skills that you'll need. They've got the practical tools for the *how* of your life with God. They have a life with God that is worth imitating. They also have a willingness to open their life to you so you can learn from them. They're willing to invest the time, and transparent enough to share their life.

FISH AND CHIPS FOR THE SOUL

When I arrived in Sheffield for uni I was passionately committed to God. I'd spent two years in Bible college and was ready to take on the world – or so I thought. I wasn't homesick; I'd left home a couple of years before, and I liked the idea of an independent life in Sheffield. I knew how to take care of myself.

And yet . . . for all the theological knowledge I'd acquired and the mission trips I'd led, I was all too aware that I was pretty broken. I think the crying at the end of church services for sixteen consecutive weeks gave the game away. It was not so much that I was facing a dark past for the first time and felt overwhelmed – though I certainly had those days. It was that I knew I could be free, I knew touches of God's incredible healing. But I didn't know what a healthy and free life looked like, practically speaking. Was there something beyond the absence of pain where I'd learn how to build relationships, fall in love, plan for the future and grow in confidence? If so I hadn't found it, and it frustrated me. Did I not pray something properly? Was there something dark and twisted deeply entrenched within me that made it harder? I knew I needed some guidance but I wasn't sure how to get it. In the meantime I'd go to church, pray, cry and hope that at some point things would get clearer. I also stopped wearing mascara because I was sick of looking ridiculous at the end of church every week. *Très* unattractive.

Sometimes during the sermons the vicar, a guy called Mike Breen, talked about his family and in particular his wife Sally. I liked the way she seemed really down to earth; her faith was practical. I looked forward to meeting her . . .

Sally: I met Jo for the first time in a queue in the fish and chip shop. It was after a Sunday evening service, and Mike and I had decided some chips eaten out of newspaper would end the evening perfectly. We were waiting in the chip shop when a very extrovert and enthusiastic young woman introduced herself to me. 'I'm Jo,' she said. 'Are you Sally? Is this the jacket Mike mentioned in his sermon last week?' looking directly at the navy-blue jacket I was wearing. I smiled and said, 'Yes. This is the jacket.' It was the jacket I had prayed for before shopping in the charity shops, and had found and had given thanks for.

We chatted and exchanged small details about our lives. We had nothing in common! I was a white middle-class mother, a vicar's wife for over ten years. Jo was a black single woman, a student who had grown up in inner-city London. I really liked her. I must have invited her round to our house. I don't remember – maybe she just turned up. But what happened is that we started walking on the same road, and our lives came together. We've shared countless key moments since then. She watched my children grow into adults, and she's the one they call in a crisis. I've watched her wrestle with being single, then saw her walk down the aisle, in a wedding dress she thought she'd never wear, towards a wonderful young man. I've held her newborn babies. We've even moved countries together, our furniture packed in a twenty-foot metal container on a ship called Faith.

And we've talked. We've talked for hours and hours. We've talked about love and life and houses and clothing and men and money and holidays and friendship and bodies and everything in between. And because life hasn't stopped surprising us, we're still talking, we're still learning.

Although our backgrounds are so very different we share a common passion: women! We love being women; we love the women in our lives and have been privileged to disciple hundreds of them over the years. We love walking through life with them. And we've discovered we share a particular passion for women in their twenties: loving them, leading them, equipping and empowering them. We know that God wants to unlock their potential, and we love to see young women discover God's grace and His greatness at such an incredible stage of their lives.

HONEST CONVERSATIONS

So because I liked the story of a jacket and the pragmatic (and, I might add, rather stylish) spirituality that lay behind it, Sally and I got talking and kept talking: about everything I could think of and also about things I didn't want to think about but somehow knew I needed to. Many of those conversations happened over coffee, at the kitchen table, at a garden centre (Sally's choice), unpacking the groceries, close enough to everyday life to realise and remember that God is interested and involved in the intricacies of life. And so the practical working out of my faith, the *how* to take what I was reading in the Bible and learning at church, began to unfold. Obviously I also learned a lot from my community of friends along the way (and we'll talk a lot more about friendships later), but having someone who was a few steps further along in life than me added a depth and richness – and sense of perspective – that I simply couldn't have found elsewhere. When I look back on my twenties, they were defined and transformed by many conversations. Not always *easy* conversations (you'll discover in this book that Sally knows how to tell the truth in love!), but *honest* conversations. They would remind me of biblical truths, help me confront my fears, lead me back to the foot of the cross, remind me of a faithful Saviour and Redeemer.

AND SO A BOOK . . .

Do you want some company for your journey as a Christian woman in her twenties and thirties, exploring how to walk with God? You see, God never intended us to have to work life out all by ourselves; we were never meant to walk through life alone – we simply weren't designed to function that way. So even though we can't walk with you in person, we invite you to walk with us through this book, which reflects the honest conversations we've had with the many women we've mentored over the years, and our reflections and observations along the way. It shares the thoughts of dear friends (their names changed!) who were strong enough to show their vulnerability, in order to minister to you in yours. It explores some of our own difficult moments where we prayed and pleaded for revelation about the future, where we discovered God's grace and mercy, and learned how to become whole and healthy and fully functioning.

We've learned that God has a plan for our lives, even when it feels as if we're drifting. We've discovered that womanhood is not merely the stuff of pop princesses, sassy sexuality and fairytale endings – no matter how much the world around us suggests otherwise. Nor is it a dulled-down, less fun version of the world that's labelled 'Christian'; God invites us into a life that is much richer than any fantasy. We've discovered that God can be found and known in the everyday, ordinary, mundane situations of life, and that we can walk with Him there. We've seen over the years that the way you get past the past is to face it with Him. We've discovered that He can rebuild a broken identity, even restore a stolen innocence. Over the years we've realised that the best way to face the uncertainties of the future is to embrace it with Him.

DISCIPLESHIP: LOOKING LIKE JESUS

If our lives are going to look like Jesus' did, then we need to train ourselves in the pattern of life He had. Jesus had three main priorities that defined His life:

He looked upward – to a relationship with the Father. Jesus remained in close communion with God, and His life reflected this in His devotion to prayer, worship and God's Word.

He looked inward – even the Son of God didn't live in isolation. Jesus had key relationships, people He did life with. He once spent a whole night in prayer in order to choose people who would not just serve with Him but *be* with Him.[2]

He looked outward – Jesus maintained a relationship with the world. He knew what He was called to do, and so He reached out to the world around Him, speaking and being good news wherever He went.

When we are mentoring women, we explore those three areas using three simple questions; those same questions shape the format and the chapters of this book.

How are you doing spiritually? You and God

This isn't just a question of whether or not you've read your Bible recently, though that is vital! Essentially it's asking how things are in your relationship with God.

A healthy relationship with God is fundamental to our identity. Have you ever thought about the fact that knowing your identity is not just about self-discovery but is in fact a spiritual declaration? If we want to know who we are as Christian women, we need a firm grip on whose we are. It's easy to fall into patterns of belief and behaviour that are based not on the truth but on our brokenness or experiences, or simply on the influence of the world around us. A faulty understanding of God can affect us in a number of ways: we can get legalistic, assuming that God will somehow love us more if we work a little harder, are a bit better. We can become entitled, assuming that as princesses our heavenly King is like some divine genie who clicks his fingers and makes our dreams and fantasies come true. So we need to go back to the foundations of our faith, and take a fresh look at who God is. He defines everything.

How are you doing relationally? You and other people

We rise and fall on the strength of our relationships. They (or the lack of them) are not just significant – they utterly define and shape our lives. So when we ask how people are doing relationally, we also expect to find out what's happening on the inside. With this question we process issues concerning family, friendships, singleness, dating life, relationships, sex, marriage – maybe even kids.

How are you engaging with life practically? You and the world

This question deals with some of the practicalities of life. Our faith is not supposed to be just felt or thought about – it is to be lived out for all to see! So when we are mentoring women we look at what is happening in everyday life. How are we engaging with the ordinary? Is God a Sunday thing, or does walking with Jesus shape how we live? How does knowing Jesus affect our finances, our time management, what we eat and drink, what we wear? We also consider our responsibility as Christians to represent Jesus in this world. Are we engaging with the world around us and sharing Jesus with others in our words and actions? We believe that we were given a purpose and a destiny when we were put on this earth. It's important to engage with God's call on our lives – wherever He has placed us.

We've found over the years that questions like these open up conversations and help us to get transparent about how life really is. We need to ask ourselves these questions on a regular basis, and we need to be talking through the answers with our Christian friends. And as we talk and reflect and pray we need to discover what God is revealing to us about our lives – and settle in our heart and plans how we will respond to what He is saying.

ARE YOU READY?

So whether you are reading this by yourself, with your small group or your girlfriends or because you mentor twenty-somethings, grab a coffee and prepare yourself for some honest conversation. Scribble down the sides of the pages, argue with the book, and come up with your own opinions. The most important thing you can do is to prayerfully engage with the thoughts here and process them in your community, working out what it means to follow Jesus . . .

We'll begin with the first question and take a look at our foundations, to see how firm they are. How are you doing spiritually?

2

A tale of two fathers

The Bible teaches us so much about God that its pages can barely contain Him. Throughout Scripture we see the heroes of faith wrestling to put into words who God is and what He has done. It's fitting that so many of the verses in Scripture that describe God are actually found in song; when we focus on Him, worship and praise seem like the inevitable response:

> The LORD is my strength and my defence;
> he has become my salvation.
> He is my God, and I will praise him,
> my father's God, and I will exalt him.
> The LORD is a warrior;
> the LORD is his name.
> (Exod. 15:2–3)

> For the LORD is our judge,
> the LORD is our lawgiver,
> the LORD is our king;
> it is he who will save us.
> (Isa. 33:22)

> Therefore, since we are receiving a kingdom that cannot be shaken, let us be thankful, and so worship God acceptably with reverence and awe, for our 'God is a consuming fire.'
>
> (Heb. 12:28–29)

Creator. Warrior. King. Judge. Majestic. Almighty. Holy. Consuming fire. Our God is incredible, awe-inspiring and, honestly, intimidating. Can this God be approached? There's more:

> The righteous cry out, and the Lord hears them;
> he delivers them from all their troubles.
> The Lord is close to the broken-hearted
> and saves those who are crushed in spirit.
> (Ps. 34:17–18)

> Praise the Lord, my soul,
> and forget not all his benefits –
> who forgives all your sins
> and heals all your diseases,
> who redeems your life from the pit
> and crowns you with love and compassion,
> who satisfies your desires with good things
> so that your youth is renewed like the eagle's.
> (Ps. 103:2–5)

> But because of his great love for us, God, who is rich in mercy, made us alive with Christ even when we were dead in transgressions – it is by grace you have been saved.
> (Eph. 2:4–5)

Deliverer. Saviour. Forgiver. Healer. Redeemer. Gracious. Compassionate. Rich in love. Trustworthy. Faithful. Rich in mercy.

This is our God. Do you know Him? Have you met Him? I

know we know *of* Him, I know we've learned *about* Him, that we may even passionately believe *in* Him. But when you consider your relationship with God, can you say that you have you encountered both the majesty and the mercy of God, the holiness and the healing, the consuming fire and the compassion?

When we look at Jesus' life, His example shows us much more than the appropriate description for God from among His many attributes. He illustrates the nature of the relationship that God invites us all into. It was a relationship with God that was close – intimate, even. It was a relationship where Jesus looked to and depended on God for His every step ('Very truly I tell you, the Son can do nothing by himself; he can do only what he sees his Father doing, because whatever the Father does the Son also does'; John 5:19). Everything Jesus said and did flowed out of this strong, secure relationship with God. And He called Him Father. When teaching His disciples to pray, Jesus instructed them to begin 'Our Father', indicating that His disciples – both then and now – are invited to share in a close relationship with God too. That's not to say all other aspects of God's character were somehow suddenly erased: God was and still is holy, mighty, powerful. He is still the King, worthy of reverence and respect and honour. He is still the creator of the universe. But through the life, the death and the resurrection of Jesus we find these two words 'and yet'. God is all this: transcendent, awesome, beyond our comprehension – *and yet* He is our Father and we can know Him personally.

So when we ask, 'How are you doing spiritually?' fundamental to that is the question: 'How is your relationship with God the Father?'

NO SUCH THING AS A BLANK CANVAS

The phrasing of that question is quite deliberate. We didn't ask how your relationship with God was, we asked how your relationship with God the *Father* was. It's easy to hide from all that that means by focusing on other aspects of God's character; we can reflect on God's might, His holiness or His role as judge and remind ourselves of how small and insignificant we are. And we're right – we are both those things . . . *and yet* Jesus instructs us to approach God as our Father. We can't earn or self-flagellate our way into His good books; He's the one who has taken the initiative and reached out to us, and now we're forced to contend with His grace, His mercy and His love. And for some of us – well, we're forced to face the reasons for our discomfort: God as Father seems too close for comfort. Yet there's even a point where Jesus calls God 'Abba', when He pours out His heart to Him in Gethsemane (Mark 14). *Abba* in Aramaic can be translated as 'Daddy'. Could you call God 'Daddy'? For some the objection is that it seems infantile and over-familiar, lacking respect. However, in some cultures, like the south of the USA, and certainly among the Nigerian community I grew up with, the word 'Daddy' was used for the patriarchs of the family, and the tone was one of affection fused with great respect.

For still others the word 'Daddy', or even 'Father', is just terminology that gets under our skin – and stings.

The thing is that when we approach God as Father it's rarely with a blank canvas. Our pasts, our experiences, our relationships with key authority figures in our lives such as our natural fathers have already painted a picture for us. Fathers come in many different sizes and colours. Some are working, some are not. Some are there sharing the chores. Some travel. Some are very present and some are absent. Some are wrapped into their own careers as tight as cling film while others stay at home and change nappies and the world. But whatever they are and whatever they do and however they behave, they will have a massive effect on how you view God. Our approach to God is often defined by a tale of two fathers: our earthly fathers and God the Father

Himself. It will shape your response to so many things, both negatively and positively, that it's worth taking a close look at your relationship with your own father.

WHAT A DIFFERENCE A DAD MAKES

If our experiences have been positive then our canvas has a bright impression, hinting at something even more wonderful than we already know.

Sally: I grew up knowing that my dad really loved me. He was an amazing father to me: full of encouragement, support and especially love. He wanted the best for me: a better life than he had had, growing up in the war with a chronically ill father who died of TB when my dad was 18.

He set the bar high for me in terms of male role models. He was not a guy who would cook or do lots of housework – I think the only thing I ever saw him do was boil an egg; he never cleaned a toilet or hoovered a room. But he went shopping with me for clothes even when I was a teenager; he sat on my bed and read poems late into the evening till I fell asleep; and he wanted me to be independent and self-sufficient, buying me books by Simone de Beauvoir and magazines about women's rights; he wanted me to be all I could be. He would cry every time I said goodbye to him. I have come to realise that one of the greatest gifts my father gave me was the fact that I never thought, even for a moment, that I had to earn his love or his approval; I didn't have to be the best or the brightest or the most beautiful to be his daughter and be loved by him.

This is such a blessing: I was loved simply because I was his. Now in my fifties, I still benefit from this fact daily. It affects how I feel about so many things, in so many ways, on so many levels that I have given thanks for this gift many, many times.

It makes coming to my heavenly Father very easy.

Sadly it's not been so easy for all of us. Many of us have watched a father leave the family home and, unable to interpret the catastrophic loss correctly, have concluded that we are to blame. Tragically, some of us have been told that lie. Others have had a father present physically but absent emotionally. Perhaps there were no words of affirmation or encouragement, or he was preoccupied with his own life. Others of us have had fathers who were simply irresponsible, destructive or even abusive. And if we're honest we may have left home, we may be getting on with our lives, but we're still not over it; we're still not over him.

The effects of this go beyond emotional pain and psychological damage. Mark Stibbe writes: 'The consequences of fatherlessness have been devastating socially. They have also been devastating spiritually. Young people – and not so young people – are longing spiritually for someone to be for them what their dads were not . . . a father who will never leave nor forsake them.'[1]

If our experiences of fatherhood have been painful, defined by abandonment and neglect, or were destructive, even abusive, then the image we're left with of our heavenly Father is fundamentally undermined at best, distorted, threatening and cruel at worst. The image is not locked away; it's hanging in every room of our hearts and minds, shaping our thoughts, experiences and perspectives, our prayers – our faith.

WHEN YOU THINK OF GOD AS FATHER – WHAT COMES TO MIND?

- *Is it rejection and abandonment?* Your father turned his back on you, and now it's as though you're wired to expect God to do the same. Your experience of abandonment tells you that, one day, God will walk away.

- *Perhaps it's silence?* Your father was preoccupied with his life, work, hobbies – or maybe his pain. There was no room for you. You are so used to living without guidance and affirmation, you don't expect God to affirm you or lead you through life either.
- *Is it the need to be perfect?* Your father is a good man, but he's never been explicit about his love for you or pride in you except when you achieved something. Now do you think you need to prove to God you are worth loving, uncertain that He'll ever be pleased with you?
- *Are you gripped by fear, shame and anger?* You were afraid of your father and doubted his love. His actions have damaged the woman God created you to be. How could he have loved you when he did what he did? And how could God be interested in loving someone as damaged as you? Even if He did – could you trust His love now?
- *Did you suffer the effects of your father's anger?* Are you scared of a wrathful God?
- *Do you think He loves others more than you?* Your parents loved you, but they adored your younger sibling – at least that's what it looked like. Now you're convinced God will hear the prayers and the longings of others but will forget you. It's how it's always been . . .

There may be all kinds of relationships and situations that have distorted your understanding of the Father's love for you and affected your walk with Him. But if we are to move forward in our relationship with God, then we cannot allow our experiences to define our theology. At some stage an exchange is required; we need the God of the Bible to redeem and redefine our experience, so that He becomes our definitive understanding of the word 'father'.

I WANT A DADDY

It can be a painful process.

Sometimes it isn't a father's presence that defines you, it's his absence. I met my father when I was 12 years old, with him having left the family home many years earlier. I didn't know how I was supposed to feel, and I was confused by anger one day, then a yearning for acceptance and love the next. I wanted a piece of normal, to feel the way I thought other people felt, to have what they had. It was a bewildering time, though I was secretly glad to have met him. I next saw him at 15, when I was much more jaded, much more cynical. Other than a few stilted letters between England and Nigeria there was nothing in this relationship; it was a farce and I was growing tired of it. I could never admit to anyone that inside I was confused and desperate. I felt he'd rejected and abandoned me. But he would never see me cry about it; *I* would never see me cry about it.

I had no idea of what it meant to know God as Father, so unless I was saying the Lord's prayer or singing a worship song that used those words, I didn't call God 'Father' for the first seven years that I was a Christian. I knew Jesus died for me and rose again; that was enough.

Besides, what did the word 'father' mean to me anyway – what had it ever meant?

So to hear that God was my Father: well, something inside me – almost beyond me – resonated with that longing. Finally the pain was out there. But it was also confusing, because I just couldn't see how God being a father would help or improve my life.

It was a hot summer evening in London, 1990. I was 16 years old. My friends and I were visiting a great church one Sunday night. There was great teaching, great worship; I loved it. But the real reason I went there so willingly was to see the drummer. To my 16-year-old heart, this guy was absolutely stunning. He didn't know me, had never spoken to me – but if he did, he would realise we were meant for each other. So I set about doing what I could to gain his attention and his affection and his surname. I was dressed to kill in my Lycra miniskirt; my secret weapon of choice, a little lip gloss. My friend was with me for moral support. We sat near the front, ready to sing our hearts out, as I schemed to find ways to make eye contact with the drummer and dazzle him with my smile. The service was great (did I mention that the worship was amazing?) and the preaching would have been memorable if I had actually been listening, rather than plotting the next steps. Then it was the response time. As the meeting approached its end, someone stepped forward to share a prophetic word they'd had.

'There's a young woman here tonight who doesn't know God as her Father. She has never known her earthly father, and she feels like an orphan. She's always felt like this. But God wants her to know that He is her Daddy.'

What do you do when God reads your life, your heart and your longings in a single moment, then speaks them out through a complete stranger – aloud? What can you do when time stands still, when your soul explodes in anguish and loss and there is no time to be self-conscious or guarded, no time to reason it away? There is no split second; there is just all your life caught up in the *now*. All I could do was feel pain. I started crying and shaking and sobbing loudly. I could hear someone howling 'I want my daddy. I want my daddy,' and realised it was me. The girl who would never cry now couldn't stop crying. Uncomfortable onlookers might have thought it was an attention-seeking teenager wanting to be noticed. They would have been right: I'd wanted to be noticed by God, because I wondered if He knew the loss I felt. I'd wondered if that hole in my identity mattered, if the restlessness that instigated all kinds of unpredictable behaviour in me mattered. Now I knew it did. So I wailed.

As is often the case in these scenarios when you have a howler in the congregation, the worship band struck up a gentle ministry song to 'cover' what was happening. (Note to worship leaders: when you choose a song that captures exactly what a person feels, you can only expect them to cry harder. Perhaps try something with contrast – a didgeridoo or something. I totally would have stopped.) The wailing continued until I became one of those people that leaders guide to quieter, soundproofed sections of the church building to continue the deep work and to prevent the rest of the congregation's ears from bleeding.

At this moment, I had two thoughts:

1 I want a daddy.
2 That boy will never like me now.

After sobbing my way through another box of tissues, I looked up to see a gorgeous older couple – the vicar and his wife. I remember their faces; the kindness in their eyes disorientated me. I could see they didn't judge the sobbing 16-year-old mess in front of them. And because they were strangers, and frankly because after my volcanic eruption I had nothing left to lose, I told them everything. They listened to me, which was amazing in itself. As they prayed for me, it felt as though a warm blanket wrapped itself around me. In place of the constant turmoil I was overcome by peace.

I was about to go, but I still had one question.

'So how am I supposed to understand that not only is God my Father, but that that's a good thing?'

'You don't need to worry about that; it's His job as your Father to get that through to you.'

I didn't get the guy. (Because, seriously, what guy in his right mind is going to find the weeping-wailing-snotty-screaming-not-that-appropriately-dressed-and-taken-to-another-room-because-she-is-so-disruptive type girl *attractive*?) But I did get a daddy. Seven years after meeting Jesus, I met God the Father.

And the process of healing and redemption began.

What can be more important than knowing the love of a father? Knowing the love of *the* Father. Why? Because He is mighty and merciful, the Holy One and the healer, the rescuer and the redeemer, the compassionate and the consuming fire, remember? If father-lessness has broken us down, we truly need all the attributes of our heavenly Father to show us that He is both willing and able to put us back together again.

Time to reflect:

Q. What's your story? Is it the testimony of or the longing for a father's unconditional love?

    How has your experience of fatherhood shaped the woman you have become today?

    How has your experience of fatherhood shaped your relationship with God, your hopes, prayers, expectations?

Even when we reach our twenties, we've left home, graduated, have a high-flying career, settled down – all the major milestones – even then we're marked by the way we were brought up. Our parents are human beings too, so even with our high expectations we have to accept that they can make some big mistakes and some bad, even selfish, choices. When we become parents ourselves, sometimes we become more compassionate and understanding of our parents' humanity. But what do you do when past relationships cast such an intimidating, distorted shadow that you're unable to see God for who He truly is? What hope is there if God has the power to heal you and transform you but your heart is so damaged that you're not sure you actually want God anywhere near you?

FACING THE FATHER

The day God introduced Himself to me as my Father was powerful, staggeringly painful, overwhelming and healing. Yet it was only the first step of a journey that has taken years. I didn't just need healing, I needed reprogramming! I'd bought into countless lies about how God must feel about me, how God must view me. I didn't know that they were lies because I had nothing but my experiences to go on, and the lies grew until they were entrenched patterns of thinking and feeling. They now felt natural to me, because they were all I knew. Strange as it sounds, the lies were hard to let go of. I knew how to exist in my current frame of thinking. What would be out there in the unknown?

So there was a healing work to do that concerned my past – and a rebuilding work that concerned my present and ultimately my future walk with God.

STANDING ON THE TRUTH: THE NOT SO DARK SECRET CALLED ADOPTION

The turning point was when I learned that I'd been adopted. I didn't discover a well-kept family secret; I discovered a fundamental truth in Scripture. 'For he chose us in him before the creation of the world to be holy and blameless in his sight. In love he predestined us for **adoption to sonship** through Jesus Christ, in accordance with his pleasure and will – to the praise of his glorious grace, which he has freely given us in the One he loves' (Eph. 1:4–6).

I had my own ideas of what adoption meant, but to fully understand what God was saying through His Word I needed to discover what Paul meant when he wrote these words and others (Romans 8, Romans 9 and Galatians 4) about adoption.

Adoption is not mentioned in the Gospels as a metaphor of our relationship with God, perhaps because in Jewish society at the time it was customary for children to be raised in the wider context of the extended family. But in Paul's letters we begin to see mention of adoption as he writes to new believers in the Graeco-Roman world, where adoption was a common practice. It was done for the purpose of getting a male heir for one's legacy or inheritance. Girls were rarely adopted, because in the Roman world women were not held in the same regard as men. So a Roman citizen without an heir would seek one out, often a slave, to receive all that the 'father' had.

When a slave was adopted it was as though a redemptive work was taking place; the slave's whole social status would change. Yet it was not just for the sake of the one being adopted; the whole family would benefit, because the family line would continue. An elaborate ceremony would take place. The son being adopted would sign papers stating that he renounced all claims to his previous family. He had no further claim on them, but equally they had no claim on him. His old life was over, and all his debts were written off as a sign that this old identity no longer existed. Papers – *patre potentus*, 'the potency of the father' – were signed. Once this was done, the father had complete and utter control of his son's life: everything you had, owned, earned, possessed now belonged to the father. The father had absolute power. He could define your relationships, but he also had a duty to look after you.

However, he could not disown you. A father could disown his biological son, but if you adopted a child the bond could never be broken. And when the father died, the son received an inheritance, and continued the father's legacy.

Do you see what this means for those who are fatherless? God has adopted us as sons. Paul is not being exclusive here, or ignoring our gender; he is applying the significance of the cultural metaphor to both men and women. We've all been chosen. We may have been enslaved by the wounds of the past, but now we've been set free, and our identity has changed. We're not fatherless any more. We have a Father who wants to give us everything, and who seeks to influence every part of our lives for good. And we need never feel uncertain of His love and commitment – He will never disown us. All the resources of heaven – His love, His mercy, His might and power – are ours. We belong; we are part of a family.

Do you know that this is the truth about how God sees you? How much God your Father loves and validates you? Do you realise that the old life of fatherlessness can be over?

WALK WITH ME . . . WHAT STEPS DO YOU NEED TO TAKE?

If you've known a father's love, like Sally did – rejoice. Celebrate the father God gave you. Tell your father how much you love and appreciate him. And allow your strength to minister to other people. Though it sometimes helps, we don't believe you have to have gone through similar difficulties to be able to minister to someone else. Encourage people, testify about who God is, help them understand what a father's love is like by describing some of your experiences. Pray with others with confidence and courage and faith in the goodness of God. Your friends may need your strength in this area if they have none of their own.

But if you've had a distorted or damaged picture of fatherhood, how do you get past what's in the past? You may take a long hard look at your growing up and realise that you've not processed your past and you desperately need some help to unpack all that has happened to you. There are some truths you need to know, but the pain and frustration and anger is so raw that it feels impossible to digest that yet. Your heart and mind are perpetually overwhelmed. You might need to consider getting professional help to walk with you on that journey. There's no shame in that; it's not faithless or spiritually immature to seek professional help. Ask at your church about trusted, qualified Christian counsellors in your area. It might cost some money, but it is – you are – a worthy investment.

You may reflect on your story and decide that you need to get someone to pray with you, asking for God to begin a work of both healing and restoration. The Bible reminds us that it's by the Spirit that we cry 'Abba, Father' (Rom. 8:15). Again, ask at your church about opportunities for an experienced prayer minister to spend some time in prayer with you.

OTHER IDEAS

Be practical

Psalm 68 says that 'a father to the fatherless . . . God sets the lonely in families' (5–6). Our Father knows that we need a tangible illustration of what fatherhood looks like to help us see Him more clearly. Look at positive role models and healthy families that you can spend time with.

Be prayerful

Ask God the Father to meet you and help you understand His love. If it's the cry of your heart, why not? And be honest about how and why you find it so hard. Difficult though the conversations might be, honest communication can help forge a new story between you and God. I remember during my uni years spending an entire night – quite literally – talking to God about how much I had struggled with His love over the years. I talked through every experience I could remember, every confusion. I cried, I laughed and I definitely ranted. I remember seeing the dawn coming through the window, and I knew that something was different. I wasn't struggle-free – but over the weeks that followed I could see that something had begun to change in me.

Be in the Word

The Bible was written from the Father to us, and in there we'll find out so much more about Him, about His goodness and His greatness. Take the time and energy required to look more closely at the character of God. At the start of the chapter you had a glimpse of what the Bible said about God. What else does it say? Perhaps you could study the Psalms and see what the worshipping people of God sang about Him. Or look at the Gospels and hear what Jesus said about Him. Whatever you decide, know that it's vital that you take the time to get God's Word inside you. It'll change your perspective and your life.

Look at Jesus

'The Son is the radiance of God's glory and the exact representation of his being, sustaining all things by his powerful word' (Heb. 1:3).

If you long to know what the Father is like, look at Jesus. If you want to know what He cares about, who He values, look at the life of Jesus. Consider how Jesus treated women, boldly refuting cultural prejudices, and know that is the Father's heart on display. Look at how Jesus treated the lowly, the broken, the damaged and the forgotten – and see the Father's compassion. Consider how Jesus healed and delivered and saved – know the Father's power. Consider the death and resurrection of Jesus – know the lengths your Father, yes, your daddy, is willing to go to in order to reach out to you.

WHAT IS THE NEXT STEP THAT YOU NEED TO TAKE?

How you are doing spiritually begins with God the Father. This is *the* definitive relationship of your life. We've learned that, though we might have once been far away, we've been adopted and that changes everything. Your understanding of God shapes your prayers, your expectations, your visions and dreams. It's crucial that we know just how much He loves us, how much His love defines us. How we are doing in every sense begins with God the Father. You see, we learn who we truly are because of *whose* we are. Our very identity is found in God, because He designed us and created us. Without that revelation of our identity unfolding in our hearts, we all too easily lose our way.

If she is to thrive spiritually, the twenty-first-century Christian woman needs to know the full extent of her identity. The Father is the beginning, but there is so much that He has done that we need to know.

3

Excuse me – has anyone seen my identity?

It's in Christ that we find out who we are and what we are living for.
(Eph. 1:11 *The Message*)

WHO ARE YOU?

It's an essential question. Our understanding of our identity, of who we are, is the heartbeat, the very driving force behind all we think, say and do. Our grasp of our identity shapes our worldview and influences our relationships, our priorities, our dreams. It may well determine the expectations that we place on our lives, or the limitations of what we think we can achieve. But contrary to the views of many self-help experts, identity is not found deep within ourselves. Our identity is given. It's shaped by culture, honed or blunted by our life experiences and sharpened and spoken into being in our relationships. As Christian women we've been taught that we find our identity in Christ. Yet though it's a wonderful truth, sometimes if we're honest we're uncertain of what that actually means in the context of twenty-first-century womanhood. We've often wondered how we access the power of those words in our daily thoughts, emotions and circumstances. Every Christian woman needs to fully understand in her heart, mind and soul where her true identity comes from. Every woman needs to know.

Still, the challenge that every woman, Christian or otherwise, faces is that there are so many competing voices out there telling us who we are, what we're supposed to be like and what we should be living for.

COMPETING VOICES

The voice of our culture

It seems that our culture continues to tell us who and what we should be and what we should aspire to in order to be successful. Our magazines send out contradictory messages. With one breath they encourage us with mantras like 'Be true to yourself'. Then you find that the same magazine is filled with airbrushed images of impossibly perfectly shaped women in stunning clothing and flawless make-up. On one level it's beautiful and creative and simply advertising various products. Yet they often communicate that we should aspire to have bodies that aren't real, and invite us to desire and acquire a lifestyle that's far removed from our reality. For all its incredible progress in the area of gender, it seems society hasn't quite decided where we women fit. Cultural analyst and marketing expert Clotaire Rapaille is a man who has spent decades studying cultures, watching consumers, advising companies on how to design appealing products for the general public. He noted that American women are expected to be beautiful but not too beautiful, intelligent but not too intelligent. If you have romance, then it has to be amazing; if you are going to be a mum, then you need to be Supermum! Rapaille concludes: 'Being a woman in America is difficult. I often joke – though I am only half joking – that if I am reincarnated, I hope I don't come back as an American woman. While I admire American women greatly, I wouldn't want to have to go through what they go through. So many rules; so many tensions.'[1]

So many rules; so many tensions

I don't think these tensions apply only to American women. Is it OK for a woman to be strong and ambitious or is she trying to be like a man, and does it make her cold and aggressive? Can a woman be strong or does that just make her intimidating? How valid is her contribution to society if she decides to stay at home and bring up children? If she is sexually conservative, is she repressed? But if she is sexually active, is she enviously called a player, or is she just a whore? Can she live a fulfilled life as a single woman, or does she really only find her worth and potential if she has a man? And does beauty have an age, a shape, a colour, a clothing size? Such issues can get really confusing for a woman. When it comes to defining our identity, society's voices can be loud and powerful – communicated by the cultural claims of our media, sometimes by the world in which we live, our university, workplace. But sometimes we accept and embrace society's voice (after all, it's not all bad) without ever questioning its accuracy.

WHAT ARE THE CULTURAL RULES AND TENSIONS THAT HAVE SHAPED YOUR IDENTITY?

Consider these . . .

Your community

Our significant relationships affect our identity. As already mentioned, who we are is not discovered deep within, as though we were one-dimensional internal beings. We are nurtured and cultivated (for good or ill), expressed in the context of the people we do life with.

We've already explored how our fathers can shape our perspective on faith and influence our identity. But actually every relationship in our lives has a potential role in shaping our identities, positively or negatively.

Sarah Abell notes, 'In families we often take on a role. We subconsciously give each other labels and then expect people to play their part.'[2] What role did you play in your family – who were you? What did others' expectations communicate about who you needed to be? Perhaps you were the oldest child, expected to be responsible or playing the role of peacekeeper between your parents. How does your role in your family express itself in your life today?

Our biological family is not the only community that gives us a role; think of your friendships, boyfriends, your colleagues, church. You should even reflect on your school days. It's inevitable that these relationships have fashioned parts of who you are. They will have influenced your values, expectations, hopes and dreams.

Q. Which relationships have broken and bruised you, undermined you, lied to you, made you feel small?

Which relationships have strengthened you, healed you, affirmed your identity and cultivated your potential?

What roles have you played in your relationships? How difficult are they to break from today?

Your circumstances

Life happens to all of us, and with it joy and pain that can determine who we think we are and our place in the world. A woman scarred by abuse, violence, neglect or shame will see herself differently from a woman whose life has been marked by safety, nurture and protection. A woman who has spent much of her life battling society's 'isms' in her sphere – racism, sexism, ageism and so on – will have a different sense of who she is from a woman launched into the wider world with respect, validation and encouragement. A chronic illness, a bereavement, a tragedy, any form of abandonment can leave us with huge questions about who we are. And even when our life experiences were positive, they may not always have painted an accurate picture of our place in the world. We may have been given everything we ever wanted when we wanted it. We may have been protected from some of life's difficulties or consequences. Now we can't help feeling entitled to anything we desire. All we've ever known is to be at the centre of things, with life revolving around our dreams and desires. And though wonderfully affirming on one level, it fails miserably to equip us for the challenges of real life. It also fails to articulate the women God called us to be.

Q. How have your life experiences shaped who you are today? What do you think would change if you had a strong sense of your God-given identity and purpose?

HOW DOES THE CHURCH SEE YOU?

Perhaps the most complicated aspect of seeing how our identity shapes our spiritual life is much closer to home. The Church may encourage us to be strong, innovative leaders in our management roles at work, but how we express those same characteristics in our churches can feel ambiguous. Gifted or not, we're just not always sure if these gifts are appropriate for a woman to use at church. We've heard conflicting, passionately held views on what a woman can or cannot do and what a woman should or shouldn't be. We're aware of a high standard that our lives are supposed to adhere to, but not always sure of who or what determines that standard. How do we express our sexuality, femininity, womanhood, in a vibrant, positive way? Sometimes these aspects of ourselves are seen as threatening and dangerous. I remember reading a brilliant blog post about how a man should protect his marriage. The (male) author listed things like never being on his own with a woman – all normal everyday tips for a Christian leader that were genuine and informed with the best of intentions. But for the first time as I read it I couldn't help but wonder what happens to the women who are being avoided and held at arm's length. In the vast majority of cases they're not actually interested in the male leader concerned! I wondered what it does to their identity to always be aware of the sense that they are perceived as a sexual threat, to know that men and their wives around them are guarded, in case they cause a man to fall, break his vows and wreck his family. Is it guilt by . . . distant possibility? How does a Christian woman who may be working with men daily in everyday life handle these things in a healthy positive way? We often find that our faith can add to the 'rules and tensions' in our minds. We want to be godly, set apart and holy. But does anyone know if holiness has an appropriate hem length, an answer to how fitted a blouse should be and what its implications are for heel height? Seriously, *where* is that manual again?

Q. What do you think it looks like to be a Christian woman in today's world?

When there are so many voices from so many perspectives in our heads – speaking, singing, shouting over us, telling us our worth, our value, our aspirations, what we need to achieve – all our hearts and minds are left with is a discordant, jarring noise. It's hard to discern the truth from the lies, the right from the wrong. There is no clear path, just a gnawing sense that we should be better than this. Yet the truth is we are more than that sum total of these power-ful competing voices. We are more than our culture tells us, we are more than our relationships have told us, we are more than our experiences have spoken to us. The Church is clearly a significant voice, and yet the primary voice that speaks our identity over us is the voice of the One who created us. When He created us, He knew what He was making us for, He knew what we could be. Our creator knows every aspect of our intricate design, and He knows our purpose. He knows what He had in mind when He made woman. He has known since the first day He made her.

UNEARTHING EVE

Eve, the first woman, gives us something of an idea of our original design. And indeed much has been made of Eve's life as a means of understanding women. Strangely, though, the lens often used to understand and define women throughout history has been Eve's sin rather than her God-given original design and her potential. We've observed that she was deceived and sought to evade responsibility, to pass the blame for her choices. We've focused on her mistakes and we've spoken them over the identity of women for all time, so that now we see all women as easily deceived, weak-willed, gullible. They're irresponsible, ones to pass the blame. We've looked at the consequences of her sin on that painful day and spoken those over all women. But is that how God designed us? Is this all we are in His eyes? Clearly all men and women have the capacity to be deceived, make choices independently of God and evade responsibility. We've definitely all messed up, and it's at best naive, at worst arrogant, to ignore the frailties of our human condition, or their long-term consequences. We simply cannot do this life without God, and Adam and Eve's story and their devastating loss poignantly reminds us of that reality.

However, when we come to explore who God says we are, the identity that *He* gave us, we need a fresh focus as we approach the opening chapters of the Bible. We need to pay close attention to what He says about and to Eve about her identity, to better understand what He designed us for. Even though Adam and Eve made choices that splintered our world, the last Adam (1 Cor. 15:45) – the one God lovingly promised Eve in the midst of her failure – reconciled humanity to God's original intention for them: a relationship of being one with God, and their call to represent Him in this world.

JUST LIKE OUR DAD

> Then God said, 'Let us make human beings in our image, in our likeness . . .
> So God created human beings in his own image,
> in the image of God he created them;
> male and female he created them.
> (Gen. 1:26a, 27, TNIV)

Here we see that both male and female are made in the image of God. *Both* of us carry His nature and characteristics. Some scholars consider 'imprint' to be a better translation than 'image' (Eden was mirror-free, after all!). We've been imprinted by the hand of God, as though His sculpting, shaping hands have been so involved in our being that we are incomplete and disconnected without His hand on our lives. And so both men and women have the potential to reflect something of God's nature and character.

This is good news for us women. These verses remind us that we are not an afterthought in God's mind; we, alongside men, are close to God's heart *and* central to His plan for the world. And since we are made in His image and likeness, it's with *Him* that we find our true identity. Our identity is given to us by our creator, our heavenly Father. He defines us and gives both men and women a purpose on earth. If we women (or men, for that matter) want to know who and what we are meant to be, what the DNA of our identity is, rather than compare and limit what each gender is 'supposed' to be we both need to take a closer look at our heavenly Father. Not because we're God, but because we are His children, so we will inevitably bear His characteristics and His qualities within us.

This is a truth worth reminding ourselves of – and our friends (male and female) – when we're wrestling with our self-esteem. It's something worth remembering the next time we are told, or tell ourselves, that we're worthless or stupid or have nothing to contribute to the world . . .

THE POWER COUPLE

God blessed them and said to them, 'Be fruitful and increase in number; fill the earth and subdue it. Rule over the fish in the sea and the birds in the sky and over every living creature that moves on the ground.'

Then God said, 'I give you every seed-bearing plant on the face of the whole earth and every tree that has fruit with seed in it. They will be yours for food. And to all the beasts of the earth and all the birds in the sky and all the creatures that move along the ground – everything that has the breath of life in it – I give every green plant for food.' And it was so.

God saw all that he had made, and it was very good.

(Gen. 1:28–31)

This first creation account continues with God our creator commissioning humanity as a partnership. Eve is not the back-up plan, nor is she the weakest link. Male and female are both commissioned to make the most of the world they have been given. More than that, together they are told to rule. God is perfectly capable of addressing Adam and Eve individually, as we'll see later on. But in this instance He doesn't need to. There is no evidence of anyone having a spectator role; both man and woman are called to the task and the awesome opportunity of living productive lives as part of God's new creation. They are both called to rule and to multiply. I love the fact that we see something of God's delight and immense satisfaction with how He's made things (v. 31). God blesses this partnership of equality that He has made. He enjoys it, He delights in it – it is how it is supposed to be. He reviews all that He's designed and sees that it is very good.

God's perspective on our lives as women is far more expansive than the rather limited ideal of worth found in our physical appearance or celebrity as often offered by our culture. We have a calling, a purpose. We women have a reason for being here on this incredible planet that is about so much more than looking hot and being popular. We have gifts and talents and skills to invest in the world around us. The advances of technology in the twenty-first century have created for us a huge opportunity to be influential – yes, in our communities, but also way beyond our immediate vicinity. We can touch and transform lives around the world from where we are. It's important also to understand, when we look throughout Scripture, that while being 'fruitful' and increasing (other translations say 'multiplying') includes having children, the Bible by no means limits fruitfulness and multiplying to that. 'Fruit' also describes the effects of our choices or actions (Matt. 7:15–20; 12:33; Luke 6:43–44); then there's the fruit of the Spirit in Galatians 5. It's also used to describe God producing life in people, and the inevitable effect of a disciple's close relationship with God (Mark 4:20; John 15:1-16; Col. 1:10). Jesus' words at the Great Commission are a further call to fruitfulness: new generations of believers.

It's vital that we understand this, otherwise we will struggle to believe we have any value in God's purpose until we are (a) married and (b) having kids. Such a view invalidates our teens and our single years. It would invalidate every woman (or man) who never married, was divorced or widowed or who discovered they could never have children. Marriage and kids are a wonderful gift, but it's not all that women are on earth for. God invites us into this radical kingdom partnership even when we're children, as teenagers, as young adults, newlyweds, parents, empty nesters, through to our twilight years. Whatever stage of life you're in, the commission to a fruitful, God-filled life is for you now!

It's in later verses after this first 'great commission' that we see God articulate the identity of a woman in greater detail.

EZER KNEGEDU

'The LORD God said, "It is not good for the man to be alone. I will make a helper suitable for him"' (Gen. 2:18).

How do you feel reading this verse? Some women feel absolutely fine. But others find themselves very conflicted, with emotions that range from disillusionment and rejection to sheer frustration. To *help? Seriously?* If you find yourself in the latter category, hang in there: we've not finished yet.

Sometimes it's tempting to overlook the more confusing passages of the Bible like this one, or decide that the Bible is having a 'cultural moment' that is best placed in the past. But the Bible is not like a shallow glossy magazine that gets outdated or in need of a makeover. However, in the library of sixty-six books that make up the Bible, verses like this evoke the feeling that you've wandered into a dusty reference section that you rarely visit and feel uncertain how to navigate! When we look at the word 'helper', we bring our own cultural images to mind: assistant, secretary, support – valuable, but generally secondary to where the action is. A closer look at the word 'helper' in Old Testament Hebrew might shed some light on what has been seen as an alienating verse for many men and women.

The Hebrew word translated 'helper', or in older translations of the Bible 'helpmeet', is the word *ezer* (think 'razor'). There are over a hundred references to the root of this word in the Old Testament. The actual word *ezer* appears on about twenty occasions. In two of these, *ezer* sits in reference to women (Gen. 2:18–20), and in three it appears in relation to nations from whom Israel sought military assistance. But in sixteen occasions where the word appears it describes God as Israel's helper, delivering His people.[3]

When we dig deeper into the Hebrew word, we discover that *ezer* is a term far removed from our initial understanding of 'helper'. Scholar R. David Freeman observes that the Hebrew word *ezer* is a combination of two words – one meaning to rescue, to save, the other meaning to be strong.[4] Dr Walter Kaiser, theologian and author, notes that *ezer* often appears in the Old Testament in parallel with words denoting strength or power.[5]

When we understand *ezer*, we discover that *help comes from one who has the power to help*, the strength to rescue, save and deliver, not one who is not strong enough and can only help. Perhaps *ezer* has more to do with what helping looks like than it does with hierarchy. We're already aware that *ezer* is a word with military connotations; the *ezer* is a warrior. This is not the only place where we see warrior women in Scripture: there's the picture of Deborah in Judges leading an army to war, and Jael securing victory (Judges 4 and 5). Furthermore, one of the most popular women in Scripture, the Proverbs 31 woman, is described in military language, using the same language the Bible uses to describe other military heroes.[6] A different kind of warrior from Deborah and Jael, perhaps, but a warrior nonetheless, fighting on behalf of her marriage, her family, her household and her community. Michele Guinness adds that *ezer* is a verb as well as a noun, meaning to defend, protect, surround and cherish.[7] The *ezer* is an amazing mix of strength, power, proactivity and vulnerability.

Let's pause for a moment.

Many mentoring conversations we've had over the years have revolved around how strong a woman should be, how strong a woman is allowed to be without it undermining the men in and around her life. Many had tied themselves in knots trying to become more subdued, more gentle, less forthright. They would hold back their opinions, suppressing their vision and passion, dial down their dynamism, just in case their personality was offensive or, worse, unattractive. But it left them with huge internal conflict. Now obviously there is nothing wrong with developing healthy social skills that facilitate good communication. And there is value in listening to others before you talk. Finally, any need for dominance or control is something that you'd need to take a long hard look at, preferably with someone who could point you in the right direction. But it's not a matter of whether we're allowed to be strong: we're designed to be. Strength and power is in our design; we were designed as warriors, just like our Father – and that does not automatically mean dominance and oppressing others. We're made in His image and likeness, remember?

Carolyn Custis James notes: 'The *ezer* is a warrior. Like the man she is also God's creative masterpiece – a work of genius and a marvel to behold – for she is fearfully and wonderfully made.'[8]

Q. Look at your life again. Did you know you are an *ezer*? What could this mean for the life you lead?

Woman, thy name is ezer

Ezer is accompanied by the word *knegedu*, which is often translated 'suitable', 'fit' or 'appropriate'. Sometimes in translation it has been merged with 'helper', resulting in the translation 'helpmeet' or 'helpmate'. But Dr Walter Kaiser, Old Testament scholar, argues against this, explaining that the Old English 'meet' or 'suitable to' slipped to a new English word, 'mate'.

Words like 'suitable', 'fit' or 'appropriate' don't fully capture the essence of *knegedu*. The word comes from *neged*, which means opposite or parallel to. So the phrase is often translated 'corresponding to'. However, in later Hebrew the root *keneged* means 'equal'. Carolyn Custis James argues that *knegedu* 'needs rehabilitating', stating that the word 'indicates the *ezer* is the man's match'.[9] Michele Guinness notes that *knegedu* means 'standing boldly opposite . . . Eve is right in Adam's face, nose to nose, eyeball to eyeball'.[10] Kaiser concludes that God's plan for woman was to be 'a "power" or strength, who would in every respect "correspond to" the man, that is, to be "his equal"'.[11] R. David Freeman agrees, stating that 'when God concluded that he would create another creature so that man would not be alone, he decided to make "a power equal to him", someone whose strength was equal to man's'.[12] Again, this is not something limited to women who are married, but is how we are all designed to live out our lives. This is how we are fearfully and wonderfully made as we are commissioned in partnership. We are not designed to be mere sexual objects. Nor are we designed to passively wait until marriage and children before life begins, and then call it godly living. We are not princesses waiting to be rescued, we are children of God with a purpose and destiny. We are not designed to expect the men in our lives to be everything to us and complete us (that line is in the film *Jerry Maguire*, not the Bible), to know the Bible more than us, pray more than us, listen to God so we don't have to. God has given us skills, insights, emotions, strategies, dreams, passions, gifts and talents that He wants to deploy in the cause of the kingdom.

What identity did the Lord give woman? What did He name us? He named us *ezer*. We are His daughters, infused with His strength and power and He has no problem with that truth.

Broken woman and broken women

'When the woman saw that the fruit of the tree was good for food and pleasing to the eye, and also desirable for gaining wisdom, she took some and ate it. She also gave some to her husband, who was with her, and he ate it. Then the eyes of both of them were opened' (Gen. 3:6–7a).

Eve lost her way, trading her potential and calling, her relationship with God and Adam and their purpose together for the hollow promise of life on her terms, a deception masked as opportunity. The *ezer* had fallen. Sadly, from that point onwards, Eve's life was mired and defined by her brokenness.

It was the broken Eve who could no longer connect with God, her Father and creator. Instead of walking with God in Eden, naked, vulnerable yet secure and at peace, Eve hid from God in shame, covering herself, now avoiding His voice and His loving gaze and the consequences of her choices. When God confronts Adam and Eve, the power couple have splintered, and are apportioning blame.

It was the broken Eve who discovered she faced an enemy who deceived her into stepping away from her place in time and history. Legacy was replaced with infamy. This enemy would torment her and her descendants, accusing, undermining, threatening and attacking. Time would reveal that he was indeed the father of lies (John 8:44), with an agenda to steal, kill and destroy humanity (John 10:10). In mercy, God sows a promise of redemption (v. 15). There was One who would come through her descendant and who would restore the world and the commission they had thrown away.

Without God at the centre, Adam and Eve's relationship was shattered beyond comprehension. The commission to rule and be fruitful was lost. Their relating to one another was irrevocably damaged.

> I will make your pains in childbearing very severe;
> with painful labour you will give birth to children.
> Your desire will be for your husband,
> and he will rule over you.
> (Gen. 3:16)

The agony Eve would now experience was on multiple levels: physical, emotional and spiritual. Physically her body would be broken by childbirth; in addition, Carolyn Custis James suggests that Eve's pain as a result of the fall would extend to the pain of raising a helpless child in a fallen world.[13] Spiritually she was now alienated from God, her life-giver, her Father, her identity-giver, and cast from the safety and security of Eden. Emotionally, her relationship with Adam was damaged because her *desire* was now turned towards him. What of Eve's desire? The Hebrew word here is *teshuquah*. Scholars vary on what *teshuquah* means. Some, like St Jerome, have suggested this word means desire in the sense of lust and thus has sexual overtones, enhancing the image of the fallen woman and sexual temptress. Others suggest that it refers to Eve's desire for independence. Katherine Bushnell, a missionary doctor in the twentieth century, discovered that most of the ancient texts translated *teshuquah* as 'turning',[14] arguing that as a result of the fall women would naturally turn towards men rather than God. For the broken Eve there would now be an unhealthy degree of dependence on men, and in turn a broken Adam would dominate her. 'The noble calling to rule and subdue the earth in God's name was perverted, as male and female tried to rule and subdue each other.'[15]

As for Eve, gone is the *ezer* with a commission to rule and multiply. All that is left is a fractured woman with a God-shaped gaping loss that no man, no job, no child could ever fill. Ever. Yet she would be driven internally to turn . . . Eve lost the life she was designed for when she lost her way, choosing to act independently from God. And if we're completely honest, many of us have followed in her footsteps. In the search for our true identity, we've tried to fill the gap with so many things. And we have lost our way.

Q. Have you ever been there – ever found yourself turning toward, longing for the acceptance of a man to complete you rather than the secure relationship with the heavenly Father?

How did it end?

TURNING BACK

'The *ezer* never sheds her image-bearer identity. Not here. Not ever. God defines who she is and how she is to live in this world. That never changes.'[16]

So is the *ezer* lost for ever? No. Our design specifications have not changed. We are *ezer*s. Yet so many of us walk around as untapped powerhouses of potential and strength. We were warriors, but we feel powerless against enemy accusations of our value, beauty and worth. We've been beaten up long enough, by our culture, in our communities, by our circumstances. If there was any fight in us, it gave up long ago. Now, feeling defeated and defined by this, we don't feel we can fend for ourselves, let alone fight on behalf of anyone else.

In contrast, sometimes we've settled for the broken designs. Like Eve we made a choice away from God, we bought into a deception masked as opportunity. Our worth and value was limited to our looks, our figures. We too were turning, depending on men more than our heavenly Father. Instead of a commission we've filled our lives with other things – money, career, status, possessions, personal style, vices, marriage, children. These things define us now. Attractive though it may be, we won't find our true identity there, we won't realise our potential there.

We need to hear our creator's voice. We need to listen for our heavenly Father. Because if we take a moment, we'll hear Him calling for His *ezer*s. He's calling out to them again in their schools and universities, among their friends and in their communities. At work at the gym. As single women, as girlfriends. In marriage and as mums. He's calling them to connect with Him deeply again, to know His steady hand upon their lives. He's calling out to them to remind them of who they truly are. And he's calling them with open arms because He knows how lost and how damaged some of His daughters have been. He knows that they are wounded, broken – but He knows He is their healing.

The Father is also calling His *ezer*s to rise up. He knows some of them feel fragile and weak – *are* fragile and weak – but He also knows the strength and power they are truly made of. They are warriors. And He is calling them to embrace their desire to know Him and make Him known wherever they are, whatever they do. He's commissioning them to represent Him, to speak for the voiceless, to fight on behalf of the broken and the oppressed, to declare His goodness and greatness without fear or confusion. He is calling them to stand confidently alongside the men, without turning, but working towards healthy and whole relationships in every sphere of life.

Do you know who you are? Who you truly are? You are not what your culture says you are, though it may influence you. You are not what your community says you are, though it may have shaped you. You are not the sum total of your experiences. You are an *ezer*. You are His *ezer*. But how do we find our way back to who we are called to be?

God knew that a broken humanity would not find their way back to Him alone. Thankfully God took the initiative to reconcile broken hearts and lives . . .

4
Old for new: the great exchange

A distorted image of our heavenly Father. A fallen understanding of our value and purpose. A fractured, conflicted, confusing – *broken* – identity. We truly do live in a fallen world, and it daily erodes the women we were designed to be. It's a spiritual problem, but because life is spiritual the consequences permeate our entire lives. The *ezer* is a fading dream. Fragments of our brokenness appear in our spending, eating, drinking. They pierce friendships, or relationships with men. They slice into our body image, our celibacy or our sexual activity. And these broken fragments cut into our relationship with the living God.

This devastating spiritual problem can't be solved by passionate promises and determined resolutions to be or to do better. It requires a spiritual answer. Only God could resolve it. So He took the loving initiative to recover the relationship and commission that had been lost, by making a way to be in *covenant* relationship with Him.

The word 'covenant' is much more than a religious term. As we understand what covenant means, we discover the implications of being one with God. Covenant explains how we are able to live in the freedom we've always longed for, and unpacks the depths of a Father's love for His sons and daughters.

A GLIMPSE INTO A COVENANT-MAKING WORLD

'On that day the LORD made a covenant with Abram' (Gen. 15:18).

If we look closely enough we'll find covenants happen all around us. A covenant is a solemn agreement between two or more parties. Chambers Dictionary defines it as: 'a mutual agreement; the writing containing the agreement; an engagement entered into between God and a person or a people, a dispensation, testament'. It's a binding agreement, a contract. Other words used to describe covenant are 'treaty', 'pledge' or 'pact'. In today's world you see covenants of law, government and business. Then there's 'the covenant of marriage', as it's still described in many circles. Yet the value and significance we place on covenant in today's culture is so thin it's virtually threadbare. In our world covenants are easily broken. Legal and political agreements are ignored, and pledges are violated. They are temporary. Divorce statistics would suggest that the covenant of marriage is on its knees, buckling under the pressure of an environment which seems to endorse the view that commitment can be little more than a good intention, until it's replaced by something else. We have redefined commitment and relationship in our culture. In order to understand what covenant means for us, we need to return to the world of the Bible.

The Old Testament peoples were covenant-making peoples. Without an official legal system for all to see, covenants were integral to the culture, providing a framework that held relationships in place. Covenants were made between friends and in marriage, between tribes for political and military alliances. They were significant, serious commitments that expected faithfulness, not based on thoughts or feelings but because that's what it means to be in a covenant.

When a covenant was forged between equal parties, such as friends, they would agree to share resources, lives and identities. The two parties died to their old identities, giving up precious possessions to indicate to one another that this was the most important thing that they could do. The two became one (the language similar to that of marriage).

However, most biblical covenants were forged between unequal parties (especially if they involved God!), a stronger and a weaker party. The stronger party would always take the initiative. If this was a conquering king, he'd give his new subjects the right to have a relationship with him. The old identity of the weaker party would die. And yet this kind of covenant benefits everyone, providing unity, shared resources and protection from a common enemy.

The way covenants were made was rich in symbolism. Animals would be sacrificed. So the animals were cut into two (yes, a gory process) and laid out on each side, a pathway of blood forming in the middle. The stronger party making the covenant would stand at one end with all his possessions and all he represented, and the weaker party would stand at the other side with all that he had and represented. The two would then walk between the pieces towards each other. As they exchanged places, they exchanged identities and became one.

A scar was made to symbolise the significant agreement that had been reached. Usually the wrist or heel of the hand was cut, then earth was put into the cut so that the scar would always stand out, a permanent reminder of the covenant agreement. If an enemy saw a covenant scar it would act as a warning: although their adversary might stand before them alone, the scar indicated he had allies who would fight with him.

WAITING ON A PROMISE: ABRAM AND SARAI

We see a powerful example of God the strong covenant partner in Genesis with Abram and Sarai, whom we meet in Genesis 12. Abram is a 75-year-old God-seeker. He and his wife Sarai have relatives and a household of people but no children of their own, a huge stigma in their culture (and sadly still in many cultures today). In response to God's call 'to the land I will show you' (Gen. 12:1) Abram takes Sarai, his nephew Lot and his household from Harran towards Canaan. On the journey God speaks to Abram and makes a huge, audacious, God-sized promise: 'Abram travelled through the land as far as the site of the great tree of Moreh at Shechem. At that time the Canaanites were in the land. The LORD appeared to Abram and said, "To your offspring I will give this land"' (Gen. 12:6–7).

Abram continues on his journey, and like every other believer he makes a number of mistakes along the way. Yet God continues to remind Abram of His promise (Gen. 13:14–15). Abram keeps moving forward on his adventure with God in the unknown, walking with God through different lands and events, watching and waiting for God to fulfil His promise of the much-longed-for child. In Genesis 15 God appears to Abram in a vision. Abram has recently rescued his nephew Lot from captivity and it seems that God is responding to Abram's fear and discouragement by telling him not to be afraid and reminding him of who his God actually is.

But for Abram it's been a long journey. He's travelled distant lands in response to God, taking with him people who are essentially his responsibility. He's endured struggles and battles and faced danger. And this God, his God, gave him a promise that would have made it all worth it. Except that the promise still hasn't arrived. Had he really seen God, had he been hallucinating? Did he look at his and Sarai's ageing bodies and feel foolish for even thinking that having a child would be a possibility? What was the point of all of this? And so Abram responds honestly to God. He reminds Him that as things currently stand a servant will inherit his whole estate as there is no promised heir. God reiterates His promise: there will be a son, Abram – yes, from your ageing bodies I will give you a son, who will be the source of many, many children, more numerous than the stars in the sky above (Gen. 15:5).

In that moment Abram believes God, beyond the glaring discomfort of his circumstances. But he longs to know, really know, that God is who He says He is and will fulfil all His promises. God responds by saying: 'Bring me a heifer, a goat and a ram, each three years old, along with a dove and a young pigeon' (Gen. 15:9).

We know now that God has not completely ignored Abram in his moment of honesty and vulnerability and started talking about a particularly carnivorous meal. Now we've had a glimpse of the covenant-making world, we realise that God has just said something incredible. He has just said, 'Abram – let's make a covenant, right here and right now.'

Abram prepares the animals until nightfall. And when the darkness descends, God's presence is symbolised in a smoking brazier and a flaming torch moving between the carcasses, and gives Abram the right to call God his covenant partner.

Everything that God owns is now Abram's. Everything that God possesses Abram has access to. Abram's enemies are now God's enemies and Abram can expect God's help in times of trouble. God lays His life down for Abram and becomes one with him. Abram and Sarai's old identities and their past die that day. Because they are in covenant with God, they now have a new identity.

In Genesis 17 when God speaks again of His promise He gives Abram and Sarai new names. In his book *Covenant and Kingdom*, Mike Breen notes that God takes the letters of His own name, Yahweh, and inserts them into the names of His covenant partners.[1] Abram, whose name meant 'exalted father', becomes Abraham, 'father of nations'. Sarai is now Sarah; the meaning of her name, 'princess', is unchanged 'but now her children would carry the mark of heaven's king'.[2] They no longer have their old labels: they are now one with God. His identity is at work in them and transforms their entire lives. The covenant is confirmed with the intimate scar of circumcision, and as with any covenant there is the expectation of faithfulness and obedience to the covenant relationship. So we see Abraham seek to walk faithfully with God, even to the point of giving up his promised son in Genesis 22 because Abraham knows that his life is not his own.

A NEW COVENANT

Think of Abram's story. I wonder if you've already seen the parallels. That covenant speaks of a greater covenant that was to come, a covenant that would include us all. Because God takes the ultimate step in His loving initiative to save humanity when Jesus steps on to the pages of human history. 'The next day John saw Jesus coming towards him and said, "Look, the Lamb of God, who takes away the sin of the world!"' (John 1:29).

Humanity had lost its way and was distant from God and without hope until Jesus. Until the cross. This time a greater sacrifice is involved to make the covenant – not the blood of an animal but 'the Lamb of God', Jesus Himself, God's only begotten Son. Paul reminds us in Romans, 'God demonstrates his own love for us in this: while we were still sinners, Christ died for us' (Rom. 5:8). On the cross, Jesus became sin, so that we would no longer suffer the alienation from God that began in Eden. His body was broken for humanity. His shed blood paved a way for forgiveness, cleansing, healing, redemption and reconciliation. He even carries the covenant scars, in His hands, His feet and His side. God took the initiative, and sent His Son, and His Son carried it all – to save us.

THE GREAT EXCHANGE

The covenant exchange between us and God has taken place. And it changes everything, just as it did with Abraham.

Can you see what this means for your life? For your broken

wounded past? It means everything. Can you see what this means for those patterns in your life with food or drink or sex that exist to salve the pain within? It means everything.

Can you see what this means for the way you cry out for acceptance and approval so much that you try to compete and overachieve in so many areas of your life in the hope that someone will finally tell you that you are worthy? *It means everything.*

Pause and face the truth

It's amazing, isn't it? Many of us have struggled for years, unaware of the truths in God's Word *and* their implications for our lives here today on earth. We've tried to get it but have almost given up hope. When we grasp covenant we remember again that how we are doing spiritually is about Him, and not about our perfection and performance. All that is left for us is to respond to what God has already done.

So take some time to reflect on some words that Paul wrote to New Testament believers about the reality of being in covenant. (Clue: if you're searching for verses about covenant in the New Testament as well as those passages on adoption, the phrase 'in Christ' is a great place to start!)

- *Your old life is dead now.* Where sin scarred your life, where wounds defined you, its power over you died in the blood of Jesus Christ (Gal. 2:20; Col. 3:3).
- *You have a new identity.* In covenant with God you can be all that your heavenly Father intended you to be. The new is here (2 Cor. 5:17).
- *You have all of God's resources available to you.* God's grace and love and power and strength, His guidance and wisdom, His provision available to you each day. All that and more. It's mind-blowing to even think about it, because you know you don't deserve it. But it's still true. (Read Ephesians 1.)

- *You have a covenant partner who is stronger than your enemy.* Your enemy has been around since Eden. But you are in covenant with One who has defeated your enemy (Col. 2:13–15).
- *You are reconciled to God.* The last Adam has restored the connection. The hand of your loving heavenly Father is within reach (Rom. 5:17–19; 1 Cor. 15:21–22).
- *Your life belongs with your covenant partner.* 'My old self has been crucified with Christ. It is no longer I who live, but Christ lives in me. So I live in this earthly body by trusting in the Son of God, who loved me and gave himself for me' (Gal. 2:20, *New Living Translation*).
- *Your covenant relationship includes a commission . . .* Part of God's global covenant family, we have been commissioned to represent Him to the world (Eph. 2:10).

The journey of freedom

As we mentioned in earlier chapters, as we get to grips with our relationship with God we find that we may need extra support to walk through areas of our history or our struggles. Walking with God happens as both an event and an ongoing process. Both are valid, both are important. Some of us will pray a prayer and feel instant release; others will need to seek professional counsel or advice as well as prayer over time to attend to issues about our identity. We don't need to feel bad about that – the Bible says that there is 'no condemnation for those who are in Christ Jesus' (Rom. 8:1), so that kind of accusation in your mind doesn't come from Him. The important thing is that we take the first step in our response to the One who loves us.

WHAT DOES IT LOOK LIKE FOR YOU?

So how are you doing spiritually? We've seen the love of a Father who designed us with an awesome identity that was lost, then went to great lengths to get us back. Amazing love. We've spent time exploring the nature of the wonderful covenant we're in, and our response is that we want to be faithful to that relationship. It's the most important relationship we will ever have, so we want to go deeper with God. It's important to learn ways to help this relationship grow. Talking to God matters, and reading His Word, worshipping Him, making space to allow the Holy Spirit to work in our lives are all essential parts of that, as is belonging to a vibrant faith community and developing quality relationships with other believers. At first glance this looks like a list of things to do in an already over-stuffed life. Sometimes we need a fresh perspective on why it's all so important, and how it fits together in our lives.

5
Training for transformation

So here's what I want you to do, God helping you: Take your every-day, ordinary life – your sleeping, eating, going-to-work, and walking-around life – and place it before God as an offering. Embracing what God does for you is the best thing you can do for him.
(Rom. 12:1, *The Message*)

It's amazing that we're invited into this awesome relationship with God, a covenant stronger than any other. It's a relationship which goes beyond eternal life insurance, but one where we can know God better, relate to Him, hear His voice, learn from His Word. The gospel is life-transforming and we've experienced that transformation in moments and events, sometimes quite dramatically. Yet God offers us more than intermittent encounters; He wants to walk with us through every aspect and area and stage of our lives. Obviously, every moment with God will not feel or be the same, just as with any other relationship.

Our covenant-making Father invites us to know Him but also to walk with Him, so that we do this life together with Him. The challenge for us is to learn how to invest in this relationship, attend to it and give it room in our lives to grow. How can you live as one with someone without them? How can you share in their identity and life if you insist on living apart?

So when we ask, 'How are you doing spiritually?' it's not merely a checklist: are you reading the Bible, are you praying, what verses have you read, how many times have you been to church recently? These things are important, but we can do all of them and treat them like a checklist, not giving God any room in our lives. Besides, as Christians we know we should pray, read the Bible, etc., and someone telling you you should do something rarely changes your habits for long. What we try to do when we mentor people is encourage them to do two things:

- Take responsibility for what these things look like for you in the context of your whole life. If you are able to vote for who runs the country, or drive a car, or choose subjects at school that determine the rest of your life, we believe you can work on this.
- Think through what it looks like to make room for God to meet you regularly.

Of course, we know there'll be spiritual highs and lows, when God will seem closer than the air we breathe or so far away it'll feel as though He's in a distant galaxy. There will be times when connecting with God is easy, and other times when prayer feels like ploughing through treacle. The important thing is that we keep walking with Him. We need to give God space and opportunity to be Himself in our lives and through our lives.

What does giving God space and opportunity look like? It happens through various spiritual practices, often described as *disciplines*, holy habits that Christians around the world have undertaken for generations. This is why believers are encouraged to do things such as pray, worship, read the Bible, share Communion. It is why so much is made of having a 'quiet time' or period of devotions. These habits create a space for God to meet with us, speak with us, strengthen and mature us. But they aren't the only holy habits that Christians have adopted through the ages as they have walked with God. Some other examples of spiritual practices are: intercession, confession, study, fasting, service, giving, simplicity, silent retreats, corporate worship gatherings . . . the list goes on. And again, these practices are not an end in themselves.

They serve to connect us more deeply with the Father, more deeply with His Son, in the power of His Holy Spirit.[1]

GIVE UP TRYING AND GET IN TRAINING

But even this initial list is intimidating, isn't it? All the things we don't like or don't do well tend to stand out. We forget that we're unique beings, wired so differently that we don't all walk with God in the same way. A practice that brings you alive might bore someone else to death! So many of us chastise ourselves for not being as 'good' as someone else at quiet times, for example, not realising that our passion for Christ may come alive in another spiritual practice. Still, that is not to say we should tailor the content of our devotional lives to personal pet preferences, as though a relationship with God is a self-help programme! We've found that a helpful perspective on this aspect of walking with God is to remind ourselves that we're all in training. Paul encouraged his young disciple Timothy: 'Have nothing to do with godless myths and old wives' tales; rather, train yourself to be godly. For physical training is of some value, but godliness has value for all things, holding promise for both the present life and the life to come' (1 Tim. 4:7–8).

John Ortberg writes, 'Spiritual transformation is not a matter of trying harder, but of training wisely.'[2] We've tried to be godly (often very hard) and we've failed. Our walk with God is dry, and while our holy habits happen they're the worst part of our day, they're so lifeless. Alternatively they're just not happening at all. We wonder how these disciplines could ever possibly make us more like Jesus, because He's a lot more interesting than what we're experiencing! What we need to do is apply Paul's advice to Timothy to our lives and *train ourselves* for this lifelong walk with God. When we see our spiritual practices as training for our walk with the Eternal, rather than trying to please or be good enough for Him, our expectations and our understanding are revolutionised. The struggles make sense: *we're in training*. If you've ever trained for something – a recital, a race, an exam – you know that it's not always fun. In fact, if we're honest it's rarely fun at the time. We get distracted; we procrastinate, desperate to do something, *anything* else. Sometimes training seems repetitive and dull (scales, anyone?). Sometimes it's painful: remember when you trained for that race and you ached for days? Nonetheless, we train because it serves a purpose. It makes us stronger, fitter, sharper, better at whatever we are aiming for. Sometimes our training will make us push through when everything within us cries out STOP! Sometimes our training wisely guides us, advising that we stop and return to it some other day.

What are we training for? We want to be like Jesus, but we cannot be *like* Him without being *with* Him. And life and relationships, the voices of the world around us and the flaws within us, will happily determine our every thought, impulse and action unless we choose to be intentional about life in a different way. Without training we simply drift, not necessarily drifting away but rather drifting along. So we train ourselves to cultivate a life that makes room for the living God to meet us in every space where we exist. In our quiet times, in our devotions – but way more than that. There is a life with God beyond the quiet time; it's where God permeates *everything*. Our memories meet mercy, our sinfulness encounters salvation, our brokenness breaks through. Our relationships are redeemed and revolutionised. It's where our Christian faith collides with culture, where our worship wanders into our workplace, and – yes, where our high heels hit upon holiness. That's just a glimpse of what walking with God looks like; words can't contain it!

But know, sisters – for that kind of life, we *need* to train.

TIPS FOR YOUR PERSONAL TRAINING PROGRAMME

What should your training looks like? A few preliminary thoughts:

Consider the stage of life you are in

Are you a uni student? In your first year of teaching? A newlywed, carrying your first child? In my university years I had a lot of free time, and so my quiet times were journeys through the Scriptures in different translations (it helped that I was doing Biblical Studies). My life had a lot of room for extended prayer times and uninterrupted periods of worship. But when my life stage changed, so did my availability. My working life and various bosses would not wait for my lengthy quiet times. My time was used differently – it had to be. Years later, life as a working mother with young children means that my time is rarely my own! Sometimes I wondered if I'd lost my passion for Jesus in some way, settled for something less as I got older. In reality, I just felt that way because life had changed so much over the years. I needed to rediscover what walking with God looked like for each new stage of life. I learned that what I needed was to review my spiritual practices and adapt for my new reality.

Q. What stage of life are you in, and how does that shape your walk with God?

Rather than wrestle with guilt and inadequacy, explore and embrace what walking with God looks like for the season you are in today.

Consider your own personality and your interests

Are you an extrovert, one who refreshes and recharges in the company of people? Are you the type of woman who loves to process with other people as she works out her views and perspective on life? Or are you more introverted, preferring to recharge and find refreshment on your own? Do you like to think things through for a while before you speak? While we all have extrovert and introvert moments, there's probably one that you return to most often, that reflects who you are.

If you are an extrovert you may find that sometimes the idea of retreating to be with God, spending time in solitude, is unbearable. The silence is deafening and you can't concentrate. It's easier to meet God in a larger worship gathering surrounded by and connecting with many people. 'This is what heaven looks like,' you say to the people next to you. Or you might revel in a gathering where the style is more interactive, where everyone is involved in speaking and sharing. The introvert may go along to large loud gatherings on a regular basis but revels in smaller settings, or even just being alone, to think and breathe. Silence and solitude with God for an extended time makes you think, 'This is a taste of heaven.'

That's just one example of how our personalities may shape our walk. Here's another: while one Christian is a natural planner, preferring organised and structured time with the Lord using specific resources, liturgies and Bible study notes, others would find that all stifling, feeling it is interrupting their relationship with God rather than resourcing it.

Our interests and talents play a role in our walk too. What do you simply like to do – art, reading, music, writing a journal? Now you're in training, do it with Jesus, for Jesus. When you next read the Bible and something challenges you or inspires you, be creative in your response to God with paints, clay, materials. Write, sing, compose. Do you love the great outdoors? Spend some time out on a hike where you are reminded of God's creation and His power. Go running with a sermon on your iPod or with a prayer list in your mind. The purpose is not about multitasking, but to invite God to inhabit every part of your life and to engage with Him there.

TRAINING HAS A TIME FOR EVERYTHING

When you are training there's a time to take it easy and a time to work up a sweat. So as you train yourself to be godly, include in your training habits that come naturally to you and practices you enjoy. If you enjoy extended times of prayer then pray on a regular basis. If you love reading the Bible in groups with others, make sure that practice is a consistent part of your life. If your day simply doesn't make sense without some time alone in sung worship, then go and make sense of your day!

Still, now that you know you are in training, consider incorporating some practices that might stretch you. Try a practice that may demand more of you, cause you to invite God to meet you in a way that is new to you. These might feel like hard work and may not reflect your personality type, your style, your interests or your talents at all. But the discipline of doing something different, of cultivating a new kind of habit, will take you out of your comfort zone and into new territory with God. It requires a level of openness you didn't need before. It's an opportunity to learn new things in order to grow, to get stronger, to meet God.

Think about what those stretching exercises could be for you. Have you tithed before – the practice of giving 10 per cent of your income to your local church? Or perhaps you tithe, but God is calling you to consider giving away more. Try it and see what God does. Have you ever taken a retreat or spent an extended time in silence? No social life, no social media, just you and God. Why not experiment and see how God meets you there? Perhaps you watch your friends go to big Christian events every year and you don't go because it's not your thing. Try it anyway.

Again, you could even partner these with practices you love. If you already love to pray, consider combining prayer with fasting (if you have difficult issues with food, fast from something other than food, like TV or Facebook).

If you love to read the Bible, try a few unfamiliar translations. Study the Bible at a deeper level; engage intellectually and philosophically with some of the issues of the day. Stretch yourself intellectually by reading some of the great Christian thinkers of the past and the present.

Remember, training requires investment. Someone paid for your piano lessons and took you to ballet classes. Someone made the effort to find out what was available for you, made the time to get you there and paid the bills for all you needed. The same will be true for you. Training will require you to make the time, make the effort. You may need to do some research for resources that can help you if you aren't sure where to begin. Here are a few ideas to get you started:

Q. What easy practices are in your training programme?

What training exercises will stretch you and demand more of you?

What will it cost you in terms of time, money and effort?

A FINAL THOUGHT: PUT YOUR HEART INTO IT

When you do physical training, its effectiveness is limited if you insist on feeding yourself with large portions of unhealthy food. Similarly, these training exercises in walking with God will be undermined if we insist in feeding our hearts badly. Toxins like unforgiveness and bitterness, self-centredness and hard-heartedness keep us far from the transformation God promised. So when you take up your training, put your heart into it. The biblical understanding of the heart is your intellect and will as well as your emotions, your desires, your hopes and longings – all that makes up you. You might be in a difficult place; you certainly don't need to be perfect. But you do need to be open, willing for God to meet you where you are and lead you forward. These words from Psalm 139 are a prayer I use to train my heart, to give my heart over to God. Perhaps they can be your prayer too:

> Search me, God, and know my heart;
> test me and know my anxious thoughts.
> See if there is any offensive way in me,
> and lead me in the way everlasting.
> (Ps. 139:23–24)

Keep walking with God the Father. Remember that you are one with Him and you have a new identity, a new life. This new life that God has given you isn't just to be believed in: it is to be lived, taking you out of the training rooms and into everyday walking-around life, among other people. Because God has transformed us, we have the potential to transform how we relate to people. This is why our next big mentoring question concerns our relationships.

The relationships we have (or even desire to have) play a powerful role in our lives. They have the power to hurt or to heal, to shape or to distort. They bring out both our finest qualities and those aspects of our personality we would rather keep hidden from public view. They are the stage for life's great affirmations and experiences, painful betrayals and poisoned hate-filled arguments. They've led people closer to God and they've sent people running away, vowing never to be part of a church again.

When discipling, we find it's essential to ask about the relationships that matter most to the women we're talking to. We ask probing questions about their friendships, including those with the opposite sex. If they are single we spend time asking how they are feeling about their marital status. If they are married, we process different aspects of married life with them. We might also ask about their church community or their wider extended family.

On one level these kinds of questions can leave people feeling vulnerable and exposed. But because relationships have such an influential role in our lives, it's important to go there. So . . . how are you doing relationally?

6

Friending

Life is partly what we make it, and partly what is made by the friends we choose.

(Tennessee Williams)

Have you ever experienced the life-transforming power of a friendship? The *New York Times* recently ran an article summarising research that had been done on friendship over a period of time. The studies consistently showed that good friendships had played a huge role in a person's health and general wellbeing, and was often key when it came to surviving a major illness. Of particular interest to researchers was the discovery that friends often had a greater impact on a person's life than a spouse, and that friendship had greater psychological benefits than family relationships. The article concluded that 'Friendship is an undervalued resource. The consistent message of these studies is that friends make your life better.'[1]

We understand that the most fundamental relationship we will ever have is our relationship with God, who invited us into covenant with Him. But our God – Father, Son and Holy Spirit – is a community of relationships in His very Being. Since we're made in His image, it is inevitable that we too have a need for community at the core of our design. It's interesting to note that when God made the world, everything was good except one thing. *Adam was alone.* We were created to function in covenant community. We were designed for family life; we were designed for friendship.

It's no surprise, then, that friendship is a major biblical theme. God consistently worked in incredible ways through committed friendships. Look at David and Jonathan, whose friendship was marked by a covenant, a common act for young military men in ancient covenant-making cultures.[2] And there are many other biblical friendships of note: Ruth and Naomi; Daniel, Shadrach, Meshach and Abednego; Mary and Elizabeth. Jesus the Son of God Himself needed a community as He walked the earth. After praying all night, He chooses twelve out of His crowd of followers whom He calls to 'be with him' as well as to be sent out to preach.[3] After three years of life together – travelling, ministry, times of incredible revelation as well as the occasional group dispute – Jesus has more than a rabbi–disciple relationship with His team; He calls them His friends.[4] Relationships matter. Friendships matter. So how are your friendships?

Jo: In the past, I foolishly imagined that we grew out of needing relationships so much. My naiveté did not serve me well! It's not that I've not had friends; on the contrary, I've been blessed with loads of them. Nonetheless, I arrogantly wondered if the drama and angst that sometimes happened in friendships were a reflection of our immaturity. It was all so very secondary school . . . I found it hard to admit or understand why they hurt so much when they changed or drifted, or how relationships could become so entwined and co-dependent. I had not recognised the power of friendship.

Somewhere along the road I learned, and now I have many fond memories of the friends who walked with me through my twenties. I miss those halcyon days when all I seemed to do was hang out with my girlfriends and put the world to rights, generally over unhealthy snacks that did nothing to my (then) invincible metabolism. We did make the world a better place, even if only for one another! Perhaps as a young adult, your friends are the ones who are most likely to know the real adult you . . . Our lasting bonds were forged over late-night chats and shared secrets, confessions and dreams. These were women, sisters, who believed in you and loved you even when you were an idiot. You laughed together, danced together, shopped together. And during the tough times, you cried and they gave you tissues and affirming words in your moment of crisis. Yes, that boy (we won't call him a man) was stupid for turning down someone as wonderful as you! 'I can't believe you are still single, either.' And the closest friends? They were the ones who were real and honest enough to challenge you when needed. They could hold you accountable for your attitudes and your actions. They would call you to woman up and face how you dealt with brokenness, how you treated people. They were bold enough to tell you the truth in love about your sin. And yes, they called it sin. Even though I hated it, I couldn't call them judgemental because they knew me and loved me. Our friendships act like powerful catalysts with the potential for personal growth, spiritual transformation, healing. So yes, friendships matter. They always have.

Friendship may seem like just an ordinary part of life, not such a big deal as other relational issues like family background, men, marriage, children. Yet it's amazing how much friends feature in discipling conversations. We process the loneliness of not feeling known or understood by anyone. We talk through the friendship breakdown that resulted in walking away from the church. We pray with women, wipe their tears, listen for hours. All about the ghosts (or nightmares) of friendships past, present or future, and how friends can define a woman's life, even beginning when we are little girls. At a visceral level, there *is* something powerful about friendship at spiritual, emotional and, if those studies are to be believed, physical and psychological levels too.

With that in mind, this chapter offers a portrait of a friendship in the Bible, that of Ruth and Naomi, seeking to draw out what we can learn from the texture of their relationship. We'll then process three major barriers that prevent us from forging healthy friendships today, offering a potential solution that, instead of a barrier, offers a building block for healthy friendship. Not every section will be relevant for this moment in your life, but we encourage you to keep them all in mind, both for the friendships you want and for the kind of friend you want to be.

NOT QUITE PICTURE PERFECT

When you read the story of Ruth and Naomi in the book of Ruth, you wouldn't have assumed these women could be friends. Different ages, different cultures, initially even a different religion. Different stages and places in life. It was marriage that first drew them together. Naomi was the mother of Ruth's first husband. But it was their journey through tragedy and loss, their return to Naomi's homeland, that would reveal the strength of their bond. When Naomi loses her husband and then her sons, she has lost everything. Choosing to return to Judah, Naomi urges her daughters-in-law to return to their families in the hope that they may one day remarry. Orpah eventually agrees, but Ruth refuses: 'Don't force me to leave you; don't make me go home. Where you go, I go; and where you live, I'll live. Your people are my people, your God is my god; where you die, I'll die, and that's where I'll be buried, so help me GOD – not even death itself is going to come between us!' (Ruth 1:16–18, *The Message*).

Powerful words – perhaps they seem out of place for us in a mere friendship. I've known wedding couples paraphrase these words for their wedding vows. I myself once proclaimed them to a boyfriend when we were going through a rough patch as a sign of my devotion (he dumped me *the next day*, possibly as a sign of fear that he was dating a woman with stalker-like qualities). But in a friendship this is devotion indeed. Ruth takes the initiative to commit to Naomi even though there is no longer any obligation, even though Naomi has nothing to give her in return. Not only is Naomi devastated by the cruelty of grief and loss, but without husband or sons she is on the verge of destitution. There were not any good options for a destitute woman in her world. Such women were vulnerable, with no source of income or anyone to protect them. Ruth is making a risky and sacrificial choice as she walks away from her country, her culture, her family and her future and enters Judah, a foreigner.

Yet the book of Ruth illustrates how this friendship is the catalyst for God's redeeming love. It's not an easy journey. When Naomi arrives home, she tells her community that she is no longer Naomi, meaning 'pleasant', but Mara, meaning 'bitter'. Her confidence in God has been destroyed.[5]

Naomi, consumed by grief, couldn't have been easy to be with. Yet the friendship remains, even in the face of Ruth's own grief and longings. She works hard in the fields to provide for their needs and build their new life. Slowly, new life does come to them both. As she emerges from her sorrow and bitterness Naomi's faith begins to rise when she learns that Boaz, a distant relative, has spoken to Ruth and treated her kindly. He has ensured Ruth's protection in the fields as she collects the grain left behind. He has also instructed that his workers leave some wheat for her to collect for herself. Could there be something in this? Naomi now looks to bless and provide for the friend who stood with her during her darkest days. She wants to find her a husband. Naomi shares her wisdom and considerable matchmaking skills and guides Ruth on how to approach the eligible Boaz. Naomi's advice sets in motion the series of events that leads to transformed lives, Ruth and Boaz's marriage, their son Obed, renewed hope and destiny, and descendants who would include Israel's greatest kings and a Saviour. Though God doesn't speak directly in the book, His faithful love for both women is spoken and heard through the story of their friendship, the power of their friendship.

Do you long for more meaningful friendships in your life? Are you tired of being lonely and isolated, or being a social butterfly that never seems to land? The book of Ruth has much to teach us about what friendship means:

- Ruth and Naomi were different nationalities in different stages of life. Are you open to friendships with people who are not like you?
- Ruth takes the initiative in her commitment to Naomi. Are you prepared to take the initiative in friendships, or do you expect people to come to you?
- Ruth chooses Naomi even though Naomi has nothing to offer her. She takes a risk and makes sacrifices for the sake of the relationship. What could it look like to take a risk and make a sacrifice in a friendship?
- In the first chapter of Ruth, Naomi is overwhelmed by grief to the extent that it has consumed her entire identity. Do you allow your friends, allow yourself, to have a bad day, a bad week and a bad year? Have you cultivated the kinds of friendships where raw honesty rules, where people can say how they really are, where life really is . . . no matter how uncomfortable the truth and transparency makes you feel?
- Ruth and Naomi's friendship had room to change and grow as they healed and new relationships entered their lives. Naomi was not Mara for ever. Do you label and box in your relationships and the roles you play? Do you allow yourself only to be needy or needed, resulting in a relationship that is one-sided and ultimately unsatisfactory? It's also worth noting that the presence of Boaz or Obed did not destroy their friendship. Naomi encouraged it, celebrated it and shared in the joy of redemption as her friend's blessings became her own. It speaks to the occasions when our friends receive the answered prayer, the blessing and the new relationship or phase of life. Are you able to celebrate when your friends are blessed, and embrace the changes that this may bring?

When we look at Ruth and Naomi, it's the kind of friendship every woman wants. Perhaps the most important question though, is: *are you willing to be that kind of friend?*

Many of us want this kind of friendship, but have struggled to develop them. And before we get there, we'll need to look at the barriers that stand in the way, and work out how to remove them.

BARRIER: PAST WOUNDS

As we observe our friendships today, it's worth considering how we got here. My friends once commented that I was too distant emotionally for anyone to get close to. I had my instinctive defensive response, the reasons why I acted this way. 'I'm naturally independent,' I'd say, and not give it much more thought. Years later I recalled a defining moment during my secondary school years. I was walking through the school corridors when I overhead the group of girls I hung out with talking about someone. They were tearing her to pieces – her looks, her clothes, her personality, her everything. It was horrendous, the kind of character assassination that wounds deeply. Yet no one defended her; they just kept walking and talking and laughing and time stood still. I leaned in and listened, capturing every single soul-destroying word. About me. I willed my burning eyes not to cry, and inhaled deeply. I knew everything I would ever need to know about friends. I buried the words, the labels, and pretended nothing had happened. Back then I felt I needed their acceptance on whatever terms it came, so I carried on, trusting everyone less and understanding why I was always the last in line, except when I was useful. Many years later one of those girls, now a woman, apologised for the many events of that era. Her words brought a healing so tangible I felt it physically. That moment helped me realise the pain I'd denied. It also helped me remember my mistakes of that era too – the labels, the gossiping, the wounds I'd inflicted. She wasn't the only one apologising that day, and I wasn't the only one receiving healing.

Building block for the future

Reflect on past relationships, in your neighbourhood, primary school, secondary school, even with your siblings. Do you have a defining moment of your own? Were you bullied? Slandered? What has been the legacy of your defining moment? Emotional distance, deep mistrust, isolation? This is the best we can do by ourselves, just to protect ourselves from further hurt. However, the Psalms teach us that

> The Lord is close to the broken-hearted
> and saves those who are crushed in spirit.
> (Ps. 34:18)

Where do you need to forgive, or even ask forgiveness? Where do you need to receive healing?

Consider whether you need prayer or a counsellor to talk things over with.

BARRIER: EXPECTATIONS

Sally: We start out with the friends our parents want for us, the ones they think will be good for us, and then hopefully we progress to choosing our own. It all sounds so simple. Regardless of the teen years, you reach your twenties and expect it to be easy . . . We'll be each other's bridesmaids. We'll cry at each other's weddings; we'll get pregnant at the same time.

I too had my own fantasy, my own unrealistic expectations of friendship, assuming friendship difficulties were left behind at the school gate. Sadly, I've had to rethink this as over the years I've experienced a lack of friends, difficulties with friends, even the loss of friendships. Many years ago Mike and I worked with a couple in youth ministry together. They became our best friends. We were having our first children at the same time; all was well in the world! Mike was a curate; the guy in the other couple was in another profession. When Mike got promoted, the other husband gave up his job, joined our team full time, and Mike became his boss. However, it soon became clear that there were a few issues we would now never agree on. The dynamics of our relationship changed, and our friendship died. The first issue arose because now, when Mike led, our friends were directly impacted by some of his decisions as a boss, including the more difficult decisions every leader has to make. It was a difficult transition to make. The second issue arose after our children were born. We were godparents for each other's children, and were connected in so many ways. But we soon learned that we would never agree on parenting styles. I found these issues in our friendship really hard; I didn't understand when they affected everything. But they did and the friendship was finally buried. Now I can see that I had unrealistic expectations that we would all remain unaffected by such significant changes in our lives.

I wonder what you expect in your friendships. Here is a list of some of the most common assumptions we've come across when mentoring young women. See if any of these ring true into your heart and life:

- The girl I have grown up with will be my best friend for ever.
- My friends will instinctively know when I am sad/lonely/upset without me saying anything.
- The girlfriends I made at university will be my bridesmaids. They will also unconditionally celebrate with me at my engagement despite the fact that they have been single for years. They will make my wedding their main priority in the year.
- My best friend's husband and mine will also be best friends.
- The friends I make when I am married will, of course, parent in the same style as me and will make wonderful godparents to my children. I, therefore, should be asked to be their child's godparent.

Q. Can you relate to any of these? What other expectations do you have of your friendships and why?

Our expectations can cause so much heartache for us, when reality is so different from the hopes and dreams we've cultivated in our hearts for so many years. You just didn't expect it to be like this:

- Your friend met Mr Right and dropped you. Completely.
- Your friend has become a total Bridezilla about her wedding and you want to kill her.
- Your single friends don't know what to do with you.
- Your married friends don't quite know what to do with you.
- You don't like your best friend's husband. He's self-centred and you would never want to spend more than two hours with him.
- Your friend had a baby first. And didn't even ask you to be a godparent.
- You feel terrible for thinking this but your girlfriend's children are horrible, whiny and spoilt. They bite your children, hide their toys and generally mess up your clean house. You don't want them to visit. There, you said it. And actually, you don't feel that terrible.

Building block: accept the changing face of friendships and keep reinvesting

Our lives change a lot, and with every change we make new friends. It can be difficult but we need to accept that the depth of relationships with even some of our closest friends may change with the seasons of our lives. It's difficult to watch a once close friend hold on to your friendship more lightly than you do; it can feel a bit like a rejection or a betrayal.

So what do you do? Do they owe you the same level of attention, commitment and friendship you had back when you lived in the same house, or are they allowed to develop new friendships now? Though she casually mentioned you'd be her bridesmaid years ago over a Pot Noodle, does she owe you that years later when your lives are worlds apart?

It can be difficult, can't it? It also begs the question: just because you found a boyfriend, got married and entered an exciting new world, do you leave your friend behind? Is it easy to say 'relationships change' because you are not the one who's being changed on? What do you think?

What we do know, though, is that our relationships change, and some change significantly as we move on in life. Some people are in our lives for a season, and God moves powerfully in those relationships in that time (think David and Jonathan); there is a sense of God's divine purpose at work. Yet seasons change, and the challenge is to learn to accept the changes and the grief that often accompanies them. There is also a fresh challenge to keep building new friendships rather than building barriers in a bid to protect yourself from loss. With new friends comes the promise of community, encouragement, accountability and adventure. Take the risk.

Today I'm married, the working mum of two young kids living in a different country from the women I spent most of my twenties with. None of us have much time to spare, and when we do it's in a different time zone. Friends I saw daily, weekly, I may speak to a few times a year. In my loneliest times, the grief was deep . . . but what can you do? I had to start all over again forging new friendships in a new world. Some married, some single, different ages, different stages, some with kids, some without. But we're all a bit older. This time we're all vowing to avoid the unhealthy snacks (and failing) and reminiscing about our twenty-something ability to eat anything we wanted without consequence. Now we mourn over our cruel and slovenly metabolism. And we do silly things like going on hiking trips in the wilderness where we eat dried food and sleep in flimsy tents in gale-force winds, hoping that the wildlife (mountain lions) will stay away. And even though I hate camping with a passion, I still do it, willingly. Why? Because even in this very different season with very different friends I know the power of friendship. It was a chance to be with girlfriends *sans famille* for twenty-four hours – yes, hiking, but talking, listening, confiding, laughing. It was worth it. And besides, I have it in writing that the next time we do this it will be in a fancy hotel.

BARRIER: COMPARISON AND COMPETITION

Comparison and competition are deadly attitudes in a friendship. Remember the story of Leah and Rachel in the Bible: the 'weak-eyed' one and the absolutely gorgeous one? While Rachel, the younger sister, flourished in the approval and admiration of her community, Leah, the older one, seemed to fade into the background. Such stark comparisons were bound to test their relationship. But things went to a whole new level when Jacob arrived.

Jacob fell passionately in love with . . . Rachel, of course. He was prepared to do anything to marry her, offering seven years of service in place of the customary trust fund/dowry which was normally given to the bride's family. Rachel the beautiful had been chosen again, even though culturally the older daughter was usually married first. Yet at the end of the wedding ceremony their father Laban managed to substitute Leah for Rachel, so that when morning came Jacob awoke to find that he'd just spent the night with . . . Leah (we're not sure how he didn't work that out until the morning, either)! The text is silent about how the women relate to one another at this point. Did Laban give Leah any choice? Could she have refused? Or did she grasp the opportunity because she was 'supposed' to get married first? Did she relish the chance of getting Jacob instead of Rachel, the one who always got the attention? How did Rachel feel, betrayed by her father and sister? And how heartbroken must she have been that her man had slept with, and so was now married to, her sister? Jacob agrees to work for his deceptive father-in-law for another seven years in return for the woman he's always loved. Leah remains unloved.

Life takes an interesting turn when it becomes apparent that the weak-eyed one, Leah, is also the fertile one. Rachel may have been more beautiful but, unable to bear children, she is suddenly forced to experience something new – second place. Leah is winning, but it is a desperate competition. She names and labels her sons with the story of a sad life and loveless marriage. Reuben means 'see a son' but also sounds like 'he has seen my misery'. Simeon means 'he hears', and most poignantly Levi means 'attached' or 'affection', and Leah says, '"Now maybe my husband will connect with me – I've given him three sons!" That's why she named him Levi (Connect)' (Gen. 29:34, *The Message*). It's only when she has Judah, her fourth son, that she is about to give him a name which has nothing to do with her situation but is in praise of God.

Rachel will not be outdone. She gives Jacob her maid Bilhah to sleep with (an ancient custom with the aim of producing a male heir). Bilhah produces two sons, whom Rachel names Dan (Vindication) and, most telling, Naphtali (Fight), saying, 'I've been in an all-out fight with my sister – and I've won' (Gen. 30:8, *The Message*).

Vindication? Fight? Is this a competition? Yes, it is. Now Leah offers her maidservant, even though she has sons, resulting in the births of Gad and Asher (Lucky and Happy). There is one conversation where Rachel asks Leah for Reuben's mandrakes, plants thought to help with fertility. Leah responds, 'Wasn't it enough that you got my husband away from me? And now you also want my son's mandrakes?' (v. 15). The women barter over who will sleep with Jacob (who increasingly seems peripheral to the competition). Leah later gives birth to Issachar and Zebulun (Reward and Honour) and has a daughter. Then finally Rachel has Joseph (Add), asking the Lord to add another son, and dies giving birth to Benjamin.

These women spent their lives comparing themselves to and competing with one another. How could they face one another when just looking at each other was a reminder of their deepest fears and their pain? Leah knew that no matter how many children she produced Jacob would never love her. She would still be second. Rachel knew that there was nothing she could do to change the fact that she had to share Jacob now and she couldn't give him children like Leah could. No, there would be no friendship now. They could only be competitors, and only one woman could win. Except, in the end, there were no winners at all.

Hopefully our situation is not as complicated as Rachel and Leah's, but somehow we're instinctively aware of how toxic comparison and competition are. And how very common they are in our friendships.

Building block: a firm understanding of your identity

Reflect again on your friendships. Who do you compare yourself to? Is there a woman in whose presence you feel inadequate, smaller? Who do you compete with? Is there someone against whom you have to win in every area of your life?

If we're defined by comparison and competition, then there is something about ourselves that we're not entirely satisfied with, or something deep within we feel we need to prove. Whatever the reason, these attitudes raise the issue of identity again. Our value is not found in our ranking among other women or in what others have that we don't, be it talents, looks or men. Nor need we find our vindication in being better than someone else. All such values are fragile, temporal and a sign that we have *lost our way* . . . We need to return to the Father to remind ourselves of who we truly are (perhaps even return to these chapters) and attend to the layers and circumstances that led us to this place.

BONUS TOOLS FOR ALL KINDS OF BARRIERS

Bonus tool 1: learn the benefits of positive confrontation

We are imperfect people, and at some point one of your friends is going to let you down. Even one of your closest ones. They are going to be insensitive to your needs. They'll say something tactless or insulting. They will not meet your expectations. They will not empathise with you when you want and need someone to stand by your side.

What will you do? You could withdraw and become the walking wounded, pretending things are normal but silently letting something in that friendship die. You could tell another friend how hurt you are and wonder if your new confidante is actually the better friend after all . . .

Ever been there? It's much easier to check out of a friendship than to learn how to confront things that go wrong. But what God calls us to do as Christians isn't necessarily about what is easy: it's about what is right and necessary. In Matthew 18 Jesus gives His disciples then and now a way to handle the natural difficulties that emerge in relationships: 'If your brother or sister sins, go and point out their fault, just between the two of you. If they listen to you, you have won them over' (Matt. 18:15).

It's very simple. When there is something wrong with a friend-ship, go and sort it out with the person involved. Don't gather a committee to get people to agree with you and score points against them to justify your personal angst. Don't make a prayer group with friends out of your pain and bitterness. Don't repress it either, pretending that everything is fine, and then become strangely passive aggressive with them. Sort. It. Out. With the person directly involved. Quickly.

And what if they've got an issue with you? Jesus still calls us to work things out as soon as possible: 'Therefore, if you are offering your gift at the altar and there remember that your brother or sister has something against you, leave your gift there in front of the altar. First go and be reconciled to them; then come and offer your gift' (Matt. 5:23–24).

Don't go asking around your community; *just ask them.*

There are ways, though, to do confrontation well. We've learned by trial and error! Some things can be dealt with quickly, standing in a corner together. If you know this is going to be a longer conversation, make every effort to find a neutral place where you won't be disturbed. Go for a coffee, but not at the coffee shop where everyone hangs out and will probably interrupt you. A public place means you are less likely to make a scene too.

Confrontation doesn't have to mean accusation, so try to choose your language well. *The aim of this is to address a difficult situation in your relationship so that you can move past it and grow.* Rather than saying, 'You let me down and hurt me when you did X', something like, 'I felt let down and hurt by what happened. Can we talk it through?' leaves the conversation open. If someone has something against you, simply ask something like, 'Look, is everything OK? You've seemed a little distant, upset, recently.'

Don't forget to listen, to be open to receiving another perspective and to hearing where you may have got it wrong too. Chances are you are not perfect either! If you have done something wrong, say you are sorry.

Some situations where no one is wrong but expectation has been left unmet are slightly different. Perhaps you and a friend were both going after the same promotion. Your friend thought it was in the bag but you got the job. Things got awkward and it's caused a rift. Do you need to apologise for having a promotion? No. This is just life, none of us gets things our way all the time, but it's worth exploring how you can express empathy and affirm the relationship.

Now in an ideal world these conversations would run smoothly and we'd all say the perfect thing at the perfect time in the perfect way and get the perfect response. Sadly, it's not a perfect world!

Sometimes the conversation may get heated, laboured and hurtful. You might need to remind yourself that the point of this is reconciliation! In some situations a friendship may not be possible; the other person may not want reconciliation or may be in denial about what's happened. You got that job and it's unforgivable. If this happens you have to remind yourself that you are not responsible for their character but for your own. It's important to be able to leave the situation knowing that you've made 'every effort to live in peace with everyone' (Heb. 12:14), and resolved not to go and spread catty rumours (no matter how tempting!).

Consider what you need to do (or not do) to walk away from a situation in peace. Maybe drop them a note, send a text, just saying thanks for talking today. Spend some time in prayer letting go.

Confrontation can feel awkward and yucky! But the more we do it (and sadly, with imperfect people like us, the opportunity arises often) the more skilled we become. We learn how to genuinely let it go when a friend is just having a bad stressed day, and not to hold it against them. We learn how to listen even though we're offended. We learn that even some of our most treasured friendships have difficult chapters which take time, prayer and tears to walk through.

Bonus tool 2: develop accountable relationships

Within your closest friendships, make room for accountability. By 'accountability' we mean we cultivate the kind of friendships where not only can we be real about where we are, but also where we give each other permission to speak into one another's lives, to challenge one another if needed. The accountable friendships are those where someone can challenge you on your drinking or the way you handled that guy. They can remind you that forgiveness is important; they can speak truth to your spirit when you have succumbed to the lies of the evil one. These are not always easy conversations, but the Bible says of these, 'Wounds from a friend can be trusted, but an enemy multiplies kisses' (Prov. 27:6). Relationships like these are not just there for the hard words, either. These friends become your greatest supporters, affirming and encouraging who you are and all God is doing in your life, and urging you on to run the race God has marked for you and to embrace His calling on your life. In turn you do the same for them.

It's hard to measure the difference accountability can make in your life. We are often afraid of the level of transparency it requires because no one wants to be the first to admit they have an area of struggle and to feel weak and ashamed. We have to stress that there's a cost to going deeper in friendships, a cost to our pride and reputation and personal comfort. Still, as we see in the lives of Ruth and Naomi, the benefits outweigh the cost.

And finally:

THE MOST FREQUENTLY ASKED QUESTION

Q. Can I have a close friend who is a guy? I've had too much hassle with girlfriends in the past. Guys are easier to be friends with, they seem way less complicated. What do you think?

Jo: On one level, I want to say of course you can, and be light-hearted about it. I have a big sister and two wonderful brothers. I'm used to male company, and I've loved talking for hours, laughing, hanging out, that sort of thing. So initially I thought nothing of being close friends with guys, they were just like my brothers and I was their sister. In addition, my self-esteem in the area of the opposite sex was pretty low when my twenties began, so it never occurred to me that a guy would find me attractive. Yet somewhere in my early twenties I felt the relational dynamics change. I'd observe a flash of jealousy in my heart when a 'brother' told me about a girl he was falling for. I didn't want to be just a sister any more; I wanted to be wanted. I didn't need any more brothers, thank you very much! And whether I had the confidence to admit it or not, some men didn't want to see me as their sister any more either. So there were a few awkward situations where 'officially' I was friends with a guy, but emotionally we were far more than friends. Eventually, one of us would get hurt. Reluctantly, I realised (or Sally pointed out) that I had to grow up.

I think we need to check how honest we're being with ourselves. If we're wounded over relationships with girls, then we need to face that pain, rather than avoid the potential for more pain by backing away from women and investing in relationships with guys. We need to be honest about the nature of our friendships with the guys in our life. What is that relationship about – really? Friends with benefits? Does it just make you feel good, having a man around paying you attention, being your date at weddings, but is this essentially your back-up plan? Is it time to embrace the dating thing . . .?

Today, I work with men a lot, so avoiding them completely is not realistic (and nor would I want to!). But it is realistic to set boundaries. Boundaries on how much time I spend with a guy exclusively, and what kind of things I share with them. As a single woman I feared that men thought I was trying to get off with them every time I spoke. (If they were single and hot, I might well have been, in my own utterly unsuccessful way.) But I make every effort to be friends with colleagues' wives and girlfriends, and often to be proactive in getting to know them and connecting with them. I find things we have in common – and I've made a lot of fab girlfriends that way.

Sally: I personally don't think it's ever a good idea, whether you're married or single, to hang out with anyone's husband alone for any length of time. In my opinion, it's never a good call. Why would you put yourself in temptation's way and be open to all sorts of misinterpretations?

It is simply not wise. It may be that you knew this guy from your school days, next door or work, and that you feel very happy and comfortable with him – and his wife is cool with it. Still don't do it. Can you ever be sure what is going on in his head even if yours is empty of fantasy? This is easy to stop: you just say no or deliberately include the wife every time. This surely ends any fantasy play inside anyone's head. During thirty years of ministry, I have experienced many women being attracted to my husband. He stands up on a Sunday, he speaks God's word into their lives and he doesn't leave dirty dishes in their sink or fail to pick up his laundry, like their husbands might do. I know some women have fanta-sised that I would die and they would step into my place, and be a better match for him than me. Some have even told me this!

Now if you are single and the guy friend is also single the question I would ask is: if you are spending lots of time with this guy and like having him as a good friend, why aren't you dating him? Why aren't you seeing if this could be the person God has placed in your life to marry? Could it just be that this guy does not tick all the boxes on that mental list you have in your head for your potential husband? There's much more I could say about that, and I will, but I'll save it for a later chapter!

Actually – we won't wait that long. We'll look at it in the next chapter.

7
Flying solo

I'm single because I was born that way.
(Mae West)

'Men. You can't live with them. You can't shoot them,' a friend used to say. The opposite sex are a major topic of conversation when we mentor other women. They're *the* major topic of conversation, full stop. We talk about the guys we're with, but we also spend a lot of energy and time on the idea of being with them. We talk about the guys we like, the guys we want, the guys that got away, and the kind of man we want to be with. Like it or not, the opposite sex are a pretty big deal.

So what happens when it's not happening? When a relationship with the opposite sex is proving somewhat elusive and you're living life as a single woman? We walked different journeys: Sally married the childhood sweetheart she met at 15. Jo married at 29, after an eight-year stretch of being single.

Jo: Fresh from a break-up at 20, I felt inevitably raw, but optimistic. Next time it would be right; a better fit. I was heading to a new university and new city. Of course I'd meet someone, I always did. This time it would be the right someone. I turned up in a new city with great churches, with lots of young adults and a huge Christian Union. The best possible odds, I thought. But the days ran into weeks, and the weeks ran into months. Then the months ran into years. Somewhere in my mid-twenties Sally and Mike taught a lot about relationships at our church. People dared to step out and date, and within a year people were getting married. Then more people, then more, until dating seemed to be the norm at church. Everybody was doing it. Except, it seemed, for me. Feisty flirty optimism gave way to insecurity and longing. Then after a few 'almost' relationships, a few ambiguous connections, disappointment grew, and cynicism, as did the loneliness and the sadness. Somehow singleness became the battleground of my twenties, emotionally, physically and spiritually. It was the area that drained me most emotionally as watching and waiting took its toll. It was the reason why I'd question my looks, my shape, my intellect, my personality, because surely, if I was OK, then . . . It was the reason I was tempted to put my life on hold, just in case. It was the place I questioned God. I didn't question His power, but I certainly questioned His love for me. It was the area where I wearily learned again how to live a life of unconditional surrender. It was over singleness that I had to face ancient wounds alongside idolatry that lingered in my heart. I longed to be with someone, but it never seemed to work out for me. I realised much later that I was not the only one who felt that way. That there are lots and lots of Christian women in their twenties, thirties and beyond who really struggle with being single. Who feel isolated, overlooked and forgotten. I wasn't the only one with a broken heart, broken over lost opportunities and shattered dreams, and – the biggie – unanswered prayers. I wasn't the only one who wrestled with feeling desperate even though my life was pretty good on the surface. I wasn't the only one who cried at night.

That's what this chapter's about. It's a topic we feel passionate about and one we feel that as Christians, single or married, we need to engage with. We've written about it before, and yet we believe that there is still so much to say! Because we're both married now, we've invited some friends to share from their perspectives too. This chapter might feel messy in places because these are real women with real stories, and life can be messy sometimes. Some are nicely resolved, some you might find difficult to reconcile. But honesty is important as we navigate this sometimes controversial, often emotive topic. Maybe we don't often give people the chance to be honest, really honest. And maybe we don't want to be honest, really honest. I got so bored with hearing myself talk about being single. I got tired of being frustrated. I didn't want to talk about the bad seasons because I didn't want that to become my identity. But I needed to find somewhere to be honest and raw and vulnerable and real. I couldn't pretend I was walking in confidence when I was actually sinking. So there were many conversations sitting with Sally at the kitchen table on this topic. Some were funny, some were tense; some dissolved in fits of laughter or floods of tears. Did I ever walk confidently as a single woman? Yes, I certainly did! But for me the journey involved facing the struggle, coming to the foot of the cross, and inviting Jesus to transform me as well as my circumstances. Because it's in conversations with a mentor/discipler that you can truly open up, we want to pause to let people share their stories. The great thing about storytelling is that it gives everyone permission to share too. So some of our friends have offered their stories for this chapter, warts and all, inviting you to tell yours – to your heavenly Father, to your mentor, to your friends, to yourself. Warts and all.

If you're married or in an established relationship, please don't skip this chapter. The topics discussed may not have direct relevance to your life, but they may affect your friends, your Christian sisters in your church, the women you are discipling. We all know that there are significantly more women in the church than there are men. Some studies in the UK suggest over 60 per cent of the church is female and up to 30 per cent of men have left the church in the last twenty years. So if it doesn't affect us directly, it will affect people around us.

Over time we've come to see this whole area of singleness as a

spiritual battle that Christians need to engage with more effec-
tively. This isn't just about matchmaking (though we will go there
in the next chapter or so). But we've seen the battle take place on
at least two fronts. In one area there's a battle for those who long
to be married but have not met anyone thus far. Many women
have struggled for years, broken by loneliness, frustrated by isolation, tired of waiting and praying and seeking, their faith eroded by
disappointment. The pain and confusion surrounding this topic
has proved to be an effective strategy for undermining people's
confidence in a faithful and powerful God. If you are consistently
unconfident about who God is, it's hard to live for Him and
proclaim Him. For some women the pain has been paralysing, as
though their lives are on hold until 'something' happens. They are
missing out on the life God has for them, not using the gifts He's
giving them, to serve in the kingdom.

On another front there are women who are single, confident and
passionate to serve their King. Yet sometimes their skills and
passion and calling are not recognised because they are unmarried.
How has the cause of the kingdom been held back through incredible raw potential left overlooked, unrealised, all because of the
absence of a ring? Other women are happily, contentedly single,
yet the people around them cannot possibly believe that their lives
can be whole or complete without a man, and these women are
sick of being patronised and are frustrated with their community.

We know that God designed marriage and that when marriages
work, transformed by His love and grace, they are powerful and
influential. We also know Jesus modelled how to live an unmarried
God-filled life with meaningful friendships and a powerful impact
on the people He came into contact with. Whatever our marital
status, life with Jesus means life to the full. Yet Jesus warns that our
enemy will continually seek to undermine a fulfilled and purpose-
ful life in Christ.[1] And so as far as the battle is concerned: It. Is. On.

SOARING SOLO

'You have brains in your head. You have feet in your shoes. You can steer yourself in any direction you choose. You're on your own. And you know what you know. You are the guy who'll decide where to go'
(Dr Seuss, *Oh, The Places You'll Go!*).

God said it wasn't good to be alone[2] but He didn't say it wasn't good to be single. They're not automatically the same thing. Nonetheless, sadly, for a range of reasons a single Christian woman can be viewed as one to be pitied, as though her *raison d'être* somehow went missing! A touch idolatrous, perhaps? Maybe we need to reclaim what singleness can mean for a woman in positive terms. It would be a grave injustice to all single women if we assumed that being single is 100 per cent hard and difficult or negative 100 per cent of the time. Or that singleness is a sign of failing to reach your desired goal. Somehow it seems the Church has forgotten that in the same way as marriage is a gift to us, so is celibacy. A friend of mine once wondered what it would look like to celebrate celibacy in the same way we celebrate marriage: to show support, encouragement, admiration and prayers of thanksgiving for a life lived well. Sadly, it's a far cry from the experience of most single Christians within our churches!

People are single for a variety of reasons. Some of us have thought about it and genuinely do not want to get married. Some of us desired it once, but it's not happened and we have made our peace with the life we have and are moving forward and enjoying life. Some women who are single do want to get married, but they've not put their life on hold in the meantime. Others are divorced or widowed. It would be absolutely ludicrous and not a little patronising to assume that we can't live a happy, whole and fulfilled life without a ring. Married or single, none of us need to waste time believing that lie. As already mentioned, Jesus lived an incredible, complete, fulfilled life without a spouse. In 1 Corinthians 7 Paul acknowledges that a great degree of freedom accompanies single-ness, and that this releases you to be fully engaged and devoted to Christ in a different way from those who are married. If you are single and free and loving it, confidently embrace the life that God has given you. It's a gift! Celebrate it, go for it, live it! Please don't take this chapter to mean that you need to be anything else, or that you are in some way 'less' than the women who want relationships, or those already in them. You are as much of an *ezer* as any other woman and your heavenly Father delights in who you are. Remind yourself of the potential in the season your life is in:

The freedom – to move, respond, get involved – not that being married means you can't do those things, but I do think being single and particu-larly not having children gives me a flexibility and freedom at my stage in life that others who are married and have children don't necessarily have. (Mel)

Ultimate freedom to go wherever, whenever, be very spontaneous, more able to take risks – especially financially . . . therefore over the last few years I've done numerous mid-length mission trips travelling all over the world living by faith. I've also been able to develop close friendships with people in different places that I may have struggled to do in the same way in the context of marriage.
(Susanna)

If you are single:

Q. What God-given potential do you see in the stage of life you are in?
How have you embraced it?

For those of us in relationships, we need to be sure that in encourag-ing our single sisters we're not so one-dimensional that we project that the only way to be happy and fulfilled is to be in a relationship. Perhaps we too need to look at the potential of a different life stage and see our friends with different eyes. We need to remain inclusive in social gatherings too, not limiting ourselves to married friends to keep an even number. Remember that friendships involve being open to more than those like you or at the same life stage as you.

Single ladies – you might find you're having to extend lots of grace and mercy towards well-meaning yet patronising people who are trying to fix you up when you have neither need nor desire for it. It's one thing when it's your friends who do life with you. It's another thing entirely when people who barely know you feel somehow entitled to know your life and your business. If that is ever the case, sometimes it's worth finding a one-liner that will politely but firmly end the conversation. Some suggestions:

> **Sally:** *I'm really happy with my life at the moment! How's yours?*
> **Jo:** *So many men, so little time.*[3]

Q. What's your one-liner?

STRUGGLING SOLO

Still, the main aim of this chapter is to help process what can happen when being single is a struggle. For some it's not much more than the occasional bad day. For some it can be difficult for a few weeks, while others feel it for months at a time. For some it feels as if they've mourned over being single for a very long time – years. They know that God comes first and that life is for living, but that's not made it any easier. It's difficult to share widely what it's like in the day to day: the lingering disillusionment, the erosive nature of disappointment. Besides, who wants to share how tough it can be? It seems that if being single is a bad thing, there is only one thing worse: being single and desperate. Still, there are many real struggles – loneliness, sexual frustration, disappointment (to name a few) – that if left unattended overshadow the life God offers His children. They're worth exploring.

Loneliness

There were days at the kitchen table when all I could say was how lonely I felt. Not alone, but lonely. Other people shared my sentiment. Sam said:

It's the toughest part of being single. There are days when I need someone to be there just for me.

Mel agrees:

Being lonely and not being the number one in one other person's life. When there isn't one other person who has committed to you then there can be a very deep need and longing that remains unfulfilled. That can be really hard to deal with as you share your life with lots of other people who are in relationships, even your closest friends.

Charis spoke of her loneliness and longing in everyday life:

It's not having someone to talk to about worries or even just the basic day-to-day stuff, not having someone to have a laugh with, not having someone to give me a cuddle when I need it, not having someone to bounce ideas off for my business, not having someone to be spontaneous with. It's not having someone to share my life with. It hurts! It's really tough watching everyone moving on with their lives, having families, getting married. I feel like I'm stuck in a time warp, desperate to catch up but increasingly getting the feeling/fear that it may never happen.

Once upon a time you went through all this with your friends: you partied together, you went to weddings together, you went on a last-minute holiday – together. But as time passed, people began to pair off and do their own thing, just the two of them or with other couples, until it felt that now they were all together and you were by yourself. Charis mentioned an occasion where she discovered that a group of close friends and their children had gone out for a day in the park while she sat at home alone. They were not trying to exclude her at all; indeed, the reason they didn't invite her was because they were trying to be sensitive. Despite their caring intentions, for Charis this moment was a reminder that she simply didn't 'fit'. And hardest of all is the feeling that you've been left behind in love, that when the couples got together they consciously chose to reject you. Everyone wants to be chosen, whether it's for a job, a sports team, a prize . . .

The reality is that we are chosen by God – precious, His pearl, adored and delighted in, but when you're on your own on a Saturday night with a bar of Dairy Milk and another episode of Casualty *(which I am very pleased to say doesn't happen that often for me) then it can feel a bit rubbish!*
Mel

The fact that most of these women were part of strong vibrant churches didn't always help. For some women it accentuated the struggle. They were tired of being seen as the babysitter for their friends. Some wished their churches engaged with this topic more – more awareness, teaching and guidance on dating, and prayer too. Others felt their churches expected more involvement from them, as though their time was limitless. One woman wanted her church community to understand

that we have as many 'rights' as the married . . . we are as much entitled to 'fun' nights off, instead of 'date night'. And if we go away with church or to do something, or to serve, we also appreciate a nice room and time out, just as the marrieds and families need family time and space!

The single women who seemed to thrive in their community found that it was not marital status that defined them, but friendship and authenticity:

Of course there are some that haven't got a clue how it may feel to be single at this age and that's fine – why should they? I think I am very blessed with a bunch of married and single friends that are willing to be honest and open about what's going on in our lives – celebrate together, cry together, pray together and encourage each other when the going is tough in marriage or singleness – yes, I am very blessed!

THE LACK OF INTIMACY

I was surrounded by wonderful friends too, but I missed the intimacy of relationship with a guy – the knowing shared glance, the smile. The little things, the simple things that can come with being in a couple, the deep conversations and shared vulnerability. Perhaps it's uncomfortable to say, but there was the physical side of things too. There were many times I prayed to God, saying, 'It would have been so much easier if you gave a person their sex drive as a wedding gift!' Then we wouldn't have to wrestle so with the fact that we're sexual beings with healthy sexual desires in a sex-saturated world. But back in the real world of hormones and sexual appetites, it's challenging to find a way before God according to His ways, no matter how impossible they seem. The women we spoke to had sought different solutions:

When I'm really raging at God about this issue I say I did not sign up to be a nun when I became a Christian! If I'm honest I miss the physical touch of a boyfriend giving me a hug, kiss or caress on a regular basis. I've not had sex in years, but I'm a very sexual person so I have regular pash'n'dashes to ease my tension. I'll take things quite far, but know when to reign everything in – that's quite selfish, I know. It always happens with guys who aren't Christian and I'm very honest with the fact that I'll never sleep with them . . .

There is definitely a haziness about lots of things, including celibacy. I have the utmost respect for women who can say no and not get involved with someone . . . I'm just not strong enough to do that.

Honestly, it's really hard at times, and it's not just staying away from various films, TV programmes or magazine articles. Hormones still kick in and exercise doesn't always beat it. At times I've fallen into masturbation which just ends up feeding an appetite that is not going to be fulfilled . . . Again, it's secure solid real friendships that help, being able to talk and be real about it without guilt or shame.

I feel really free to be walking in purity and freedom in a way that really blesses God because I am honouring Him with my sexuality by remaining celibate. I am not the woman I used to be: I've been radically transformed by God and I am grateful for that! At times I feel patronised by people, more people who are not Christians (maybe they are just more honest about it?), who just think you're a bit of a saddo because you don't have sex with anyone. It's almost a bit like 'I have sex therefore I am' – it can almost feel like you don't have anything to contribute because there's this whole life experience that is massively important and you aren't part of it.

This one is difficult. I've got a friend who asked me if it's a sin to use a vibrator. I still don't know the answer but yes, sometimes one can relate to Samantha out of Sex in the City and want to be that liberal! On the days that I feel vulnerable I try to avoid being round a guy that could lead to bad situations.

Q. Do you identify with any of these comments?

How do you handle celibacy in a sexually saturated world?

WALKING WITH GOD IN IT ALL

As I said earlier, processing being single was the area where I learned afresh to get to grips with what it meant to follow Jesus, even if it meant I didn't get what I wanted. Was He faithful or forgetful? Kind or cruel? There were some days I wasn't sure. The Proverbs writer notes:

> Hope deferred makes the heart sick,
> but a longing fulfilled is a tree of life.
> (Prov. 13:12)

The Message paraphrases 'hope deferred' as 'unrelenting disappointment'. I could identify with that. I had expectations: a magic age when I'd settle down, the way it would happen, the way I would know my life was about to change. I was hugely disappointed when life didn't go my (note *my*, not God's) way. I had no plan B because I'd invested a lot of prayer in God delivering on my plan A. My heart – and note that the biblical word for heart meant more than feelings but also encompassed thoughts, will, intellect, longing – was sick for a while and I had to work it through. Did my Father love me? Had He forgotten me? Is God faithful and true after all, or is that just for someone else? Heartsickness afflicts us all when our expectations for our careers, our homes, our friends, our health, our love life – anything – are left unfulfilled. It brings us to our knees and causes us to examine our fears:

I used to see being single as just the phase I was in. Now I worry that it's what my life will be like for ever and that scares the s**t out of me.

I see friends in difficult marriages and know marriage is not the be all and end all. I have hope and trust that God has it covered but there are days when I struggle. The single biggest effect on my faith is trusting God and not letting my being unmarried/not dating affect my relationship with God or the ministry He has called me to.

In many ways, in one sense it deepens the intimacy I have, because Jesus has to be my all. He is the one I go everywhere with, who will travel the world with me. I need to fully rely on Him as He is the only one I can fully rely on being there to walk through life with me. Yet my dream has always been to marry and have children, and this feels like a delay. I have to constantly choose to believe that God is still faithful, and to still be able to recognise and appreciate the amazing gifts He does put in my life.

How does unrelenting disappointment (concerning singleness, or anything else, for that matter) affect your life? Has it caused you to walk away from God, to question His love, to create your own solutions? Do you still know He loves you?

Alongside facing personal disappointment, walking with God during this period of my life brought me a huge wake-up call. A friend reminded me once that I was not single because no one was interested. I was single because I'd made a choice out of my walk with God to only date Christian men. This was a consequence, a cost of following Jesus. Her comments gave me a sense of perspective and challenge. Jesus spoke regularly about the cost of being a disciple: 'Whoever wants to be my disciple must deny themselves and take up their cross and follow me' (Mark 8:34). Walking with God was a path to forgiveness and eternal life, but the journey was via the cross. Could I deny my desires and longing, my frustrations and tears, because I loved Jesus more? Did I believe that knowing

God was more important than getting married? Would I follow Him even if I didn't get what I wanted? The questions illuminated lots of attitudes in my heart. My dreams and desires had become my rights. And quite self-righteous ones too!

I thought: 'I've been a good girl for you, Jesus! I've not worn any inappropriate clothing for a long time now! And I don't drink. And I've not had any cheeky snogs in nightclubs or anything. You can rely on me – so what's taking You so long?'

I'd forgotten that I'd given my life over to my covenant partner, that my life was His now, that I'd surrendered everything to Him. Well, except this area that I kept on taking back. And the truth was, my ideals at times became my idol. While there was no wooden statue, my priorities had begun to reshape themselves around what I felt was the most important thing I needed in my life.

So over time and sometimes through the tears I learned to surrender my life to the Lord again, this dream and every other one, all of life's disappointments and desires. I learned that His steady hand on my life completed me. I didn't stop praying about it, or even having bad days; I had friends who would pray with me and for me. But I learned to seek first the kingdom (Matt. 6:33) – God's rule in my life – and embrace the life He had for me. I discovered that life with God wasn't on hold until there was a ring on my finger: there was a life I wasn't living. I had a lot to learn still about how to move forward on the singleness stuff, but in the meantime taking hold of my life was a strange exhilarating sensation. It was a bit like soaring. It was a gift.

ARE YOU SOARING OR STRUGGLING?

Where do we go from here? If you're soaring solo, then grab hold of your strap line and fly. Don't allow culture's expectations to tame what God has placed in your heart. If you're struggling, take an honest look at how you walk with God in it all. Is there a need to stop and surrender?

But it doesn't stop there, because even as we sort through our emotions and frustrations, realign our priorities, we still need to move forward in some way. You are not as powerless as you might feel. Being real and honest is important but it's a great starting point, not an end in itself. We follow a God who is loving, powerful and life-transforming. So if you want to change your life in this area and move forward, what happens now?

8

Dates and mates: in search of Mr Right

Some people are settling down, some people are settling and some people refuse to settle for anything less than butterflies.
(Sex and the City)

In the animated film *Shrek the Third*, there's a scene where the dastardly Prince Charming locks Princess Fiona and her fellow princess friends, Rapunzel, Snow White, Sleeping Beauty and Cinderella, in a dungeon to prevent them from foiling his plans to become king. Fiona realises that it's time for action and tries to gather the women for the cause. Snow White delivers the command to the women 'Assume the position!' and they all adopt bizarre passive postures. Perturbed, Fiona asks what is going on. Their response? 'We're waiting to be rescued.' They've all adopted the position they were in when their princes rescued them in their fairytales . . .

If there is anywhere in women's journeys where we seem to buy into the fairytale-princess type ideals it's in the area of falling in love. Even the most logical, princess-culture-hating, pragmatic type of woman readily becomes a helpless damsel in distress, longing for a way out of this dark dank dungeon called singleness, believing that only a *fine* Prince-of-God can set her free. But more often than not, *the only things that hold our gorgeous damsel captive are her own mindset and her own inactivity on the matter, and the keys to both are in her own hands.* Sometimes the problem isn't to do with the lack of men, the demands of our job and our calling, the lack of initiative the church displays on behalf of its unmarried members, the lack of friends understanding where we are. Sometimes the problem is much closer to home. Sometimes the problem is us.

Now, you might want to kill us for that statement, call us insensitive, smug or hopelessly out of touch. But before you throw the book down and walk away, hold on for a moment. When we've wanted and sacrificed and prayed towards something for a long time, to hear that *our* actions have been a part of the problem is the kind of bitter pill that is not only difficult to swallow, it gets stuck in your throat. Such a statement feels offensive, especially in the area of being single. We are not saying that the issues mentioned above haven't had any effect on your current situation. But we do want to take this opportunity to talk to you woman to woman, *ezer* to *ezer*. Yes, this is a difficult, even painful, situation for many of us. Still, we don't easily acknowledge that we might bear some responsibility for our situation too. If we are going to move forward we will need to face *all* the facts, including those about ourselves, even if they are a bit brutal and painful at times.

We've found as we've mentored people that while there are lots of great books out there on relationships and marriage and wonderful resources on parenting, there's actually not so much on how to get together with someone. So our aim in this chapter is twofold:

- to reflect on some of our ideas and approaches to relationships that, while well intentioned, often hold us back and get in the way of the very thing we long for;
- to give some very practical suggestions of how to be proactive in this area of your life in a healthy way (yes, we are going to ask you to do something!).

Are you ready to go there? When I used to process this area of my life with Sally, it was tough. I argued with her every step of the way. But the great thing about the process was that it forced me to face myself and my weakness. It was both disconcerting and empowering because I was no longer a victim of my circumstances. Eventually, life looked a lot more like fun!

APPROACHES THAT HOLD US BACK

There are a number of positions we can take on the relationship thing that, instead of helping us, can actually hinder us. These are a few that we've seen come up regularly:

The well-fashioned fairytale fantasy

It seems that we all want to be swept off our feet by God's answer to Prince Charming. We draw up a very detailed list or description of what he will be like, so that we are able to recognise him when he enters our lives. Some of it is that we'd simply like our relationships to be straightforward and stress-free, a wonder-filled alternative to the messiness that often accompanies our previous experiences. Sometimes it reflects a desire to avoid the risks that come with getting out there. For some of us it's the steady diet of fairytales, chick flicks, chick lit, of late-night chats with the sisterhood where we created a composite Mr Right made up of all the men we know and the odd movie star. In one sense those girly nights are just entertaining and fun, great for a laugh. Not so ideal is when all those ideas somehow drift into our theology and expectation of the right kind of person to settle down with; when they shape our expectations of how we'll meet a guy, settle down and get married. We conclude that the perfect match (and for some broken reason nothing less than *perfect* will do) is somehow discovered, just happens.

We are *not* suggesting an end to girls' nights with a movie! What we are saying is that we need to critique where we get our ideas on a suitable match from. The ideal man you've made up from various guys and TV personalities and worship leaders and musicians is not real. He – well, it – is a fantasy. Fantasies sound fluffy and light but in some cases can be utterly addictive. The fantasy feels so good, so right, ticks all the right boxes. The ordinary guy in church is a poor contender against the rock star wattage of the fantasy. It makes us unable to see the guys in our community for who they truly are: they can never measure up to the idol – I mean ideal – that we've fallen in love with in our hearts. We sometimes judge guys or other women who wrestle with pornography, for how much it objectifies and demeans people. We may not be fantasising about sex, but fantasy can still objectify and demean. How do we walk away from it? We need to pray but also practically engage with reality, which we'll explore later.

Waiting for The One

Some of us have invested a lot of emotional energy in deliberately choosing to wait for one person to come along. And not just one person, but The One Person. We've rationalised it in a number of ways. We're done with dating and we want to invest our energies more specifically. We've drawn strength from verses like 'Wait for the LORD; be strong and take heart and wait for the LORD' (Ps. 27:14) and concluded that the best way is to wait and see what God will do. We insist that waiting is not passive but a chance to prepare ourselves for meeting the right guy, or working out what is right to want and right to need. We talk and pray with friends, supporting each other. We concede that there are times we feel despondent, powerless and even a little bored. But in the end we and our girlfriends truly believe that the Lord will honour the waiting and the sacrifice with an *amazing* guy, as though the longer we wait, the more we deserve a better, more incredible man, in compensation.

Is there anything wrong with waiting? Not necessarily. There are times when it's good for those of us who have been so defined by being with a guy to fly and soar solo for a while. There we're reminded of our worth and our potential and it's incredibly productive. But it's important to note that many of us consider waiting as doing nothing and disengaging, rather than the process of active engagement with God that we see in the scriptural understanding of waiting. *Qavah* (from 'wait' in Psalm 27) can mean to wait, to look for, to wait expectantly. Rather than passive disengagement, it's more like a waiter actively engaging with a customer and making recommendations! If we are looking for the Lord to help us find a husband, do we expect to work out who that person might be without actually relating to any men? Perhaps the other issue with waiting is the idea of waiting for The One, your soul mate. The soul mate is the ancient idea of one soul in two separated pieces, incomplete and not at peace until they meet one another again and are united. The soul mate suggests that there is one person out there whose soul completes yours. The ideas of the soul mate are found in Ancient Greek mythology and ancient spiritualities, movies and music, but not in Christianity. Most marriages we see in the Bible are arranged. There is, however, one person out there who fully 100 per cent gets you and completes you; His name is Jesus. But beyond that we're all just everyday human beings! No man or woman could ever match His greatness.

Waiting for someone better

Some of us have a different reason for our waiting. We've been interested in a few guys, perhaps even gone out with one or two. But we're waiting for something *better*. Sometimes better is a composite of the men we've previously dated. Sometimes better is about meeting someone at a different time in our lives, when we're less busy with work, when other friends are dating too. Sometimes better is about someone who shares our passion and calling. Sometimes better is a way to hide from the vulnerability and fear that dating brings, the changes in our friendship group, the challenge to our overworking, the risk, the change, the unknown.

'A guy has to ask me out'

Some of us feel very strongly about this. If he's a man, then men should do the asking. Of course we want to be asked out on a date, it's fun and affirming. Yet we believe this first step has been totally over-spiritualised. We are often told, 'How can he lead in marriage if he can't ask me out on a date?' If we are going to get all scriptural about it, check out Ruth 3:7–9, where our girl Ruth initiates her relationship with Boaz. Judging the measure of a man's strength and character by how he approaches you doesn't give him a chance to have a shy or insecure day. When you are sitting there with your ten girlfriends in a row at church, he might find you all – though gorgeous – a little intimidating. More to the point sometimes, though, waiting to be pursued sounds a little bit like the damsel in distress assuming her position! And don't forget, not every guy who pursues you is a guy you need to be spending time with. Some (like some women) just enjoy the challenge, the thrill of the chase. If the pursuit is your only proviso, you might want to change your standards.

The prophetic word

Some of us believe we've been given a specific word about who we will marry. We know his name, we know all about him (I hate to be crass, but he's often a worship leader). We're not even sure we like him, we just feel it's 'meant to be'. It can be a truly confusing experience for people who find themselves in this position. Do you hold on to the word or let go? The Bible calls us to test everything, so it's worth being accountable about it. Accountability is vital here because it's easy to start fantasising in your head and calling it prophecy. If God's said it, it must be true, and you get to opt out of the fears and insecurities that are found in dating. A friend can bring accountability and, in a number of cases, a much-needed dose of reality.

'I can't help what I'm attracted to'

This is another common approach: we don't want to date outside our 'type', whatever that type may be. But are you willing to miss an incredible opportunity because his hair is brown, not blond, or he's an introvert, not an extrovert? Because he's not a great dancer? Because he's two years younger instead of your ideal two years older? It's true that to some extent we can't always help what we're attracted to, for all kinds of reasons. Sometimes we're attracted to men who are unhealthy for us and we need to ask the Lord to change our attractions. When reflecting on her relationships the actress Laura Linney realised: '*Charisma is not character.* A magnetic personality doesn't necessarily indicate a good heart. I'd always assumed they went hand in hand.'[1]

Q. Would you be willing to try something new . . .

BUT WHAT ABOUT . . .

It's highly probable that any woman reading this book will know someone (or someone who knows someone) who met her husband through any of the means we've just critiqued! She wrote a list and God provided, she waited and it was love at first sight. She waited for someone better, the man who pursued her is amazing, or the prophetic word was 100 per cent accurate. But there are also many more of us who hold on to the above views out of fear and insecurity, with a few worldly ideals thrown in, and are going around in circles. Slowly. (Remember when we looked at comparison earlier on?) We say we want God's best but judge people in the way we hate to be judged. We want these amazing men, but are we amazing women? Are you prepared to be judged by the same standards you use? Is a man allowed to ask for a woman with a huge inheritance, no PMS, a high sex drive and a speedy metabolism that keeps her svelte even after she's borne him four sons in a row? After all, he can't help what he is attracted to . . . The men in our hearts will always be preferable to the men in our lives at first glance. Ordinary never seems as cool as amazing. We're simply saying we need to be aware that there are lots of ways that God brings people into our lives, and they are no less God-given just because it all seems very ordinary. In the end you will not care how you met the man you married, and there is no perfect formula. We don't want you to miss out on wonderful relationships because of shallow values or wounds or lines from music and movies that are great entertainment but not your guide to life. Besides, if we broaden our options perhaps we might broaden the number of opportunities we have, which is no bad thing.

Q. Where do you need to change your approach or expectations of meeting a suitable guy?

Laura Linney continued: 'It was easy and natural for me – especially in my youth – to overvalue a light-up-the-room personality. But now I realise I can't expect a friendship or romance to flourish if the person hasn't demonstrated strong character. Traits like humility, courage, and empathy are easily overlooked – but it's immensely important to find them in your closest relationships.'[2]

We may have had a lot of ideas, ideals and idols to get rid of. What are some basic values that actually do matter when looking to form a relationship?

Some suggestions:

- Does he love Jesus?
- Is he involved in the local church?
- What do people I respect say about him?
- What do I observe in how he relates to people?
- Does he have a job?
- Is he someone committed to growing and maturing with God?
- Is he a kind person?

What other things do you think are genuinely important?

SALLY'S ADVICE

Be proactive

Sometimes it is helpful to remember that this is a battle, instead of just assuming it will happen. Clearly it is much better for Satan to keep you distracted or passive in this area than for you to approach it like it is: a frontier that needs to be won. So many times I have noticed that young women believe they have so much time on their hands that they fail to really engage in the process. They invest many hours on their education, on ministry, on friends, but significantly less time on actually dating, even though they sincerely believe that marriage is a significant part of their future with God. It is really good to keep on getting on with your life while waiting to meet someone to share it with, but it is good also to be honest with yourself, and another person to whom you will be accountable, about how much time, effort and money you are actually spending on finding a husband. Somehow people believe it will just happen. They believe they will just stumble across their spouse while at uni or at the grocery store. When this doesn't happen they quickly become disillusioned and bury themselves in other activities.

Get dating!

If you want to move forward you are going to have to get back out there. Get to know some men at your church, hang out in groups. But don't enter the friends zone and get stuck there. Dating is a great way to get to know a guy better and see if it could go anywhere. It moves you from inertia to being proactive about this important area of your life. When Mike and I taught on dating at our church we gave a few basic principles and ground rules for our community. Here's a summary, peppered with a few examples!

- Dating is a good thing, and it's just the first step. If there is someone in your group that you would like to get to know better, go on a date with them.
- Dating is not an invitation to get married. What girls have to realise is that most guys are afraid of dating because they think they are actually having to commit to far more than a couple of 'let's get to know each other' times. So, re conversations on your first date: don't discuss marriage. Do not start naming your imaginary children.
- No physical contact on first dates. Try getting to know someone without touching. It can be done.
- It is OK for a nice Christian girl to ask a guy out on a date. In fact, it's necessary sometimes because guys can be a bit dense. Asking a guy out on a date does not mean he will never be a leader and that you have somehow taken that away from him because you asked him first! Let's keep some perspective. You did not emasculate him, nor did you steal his God-given identity. You invited him for a coffee. It's just that a lot of really good guys are not very good at seeing the lovely young lady who's right in front of them, or are actually slightly afraid to ask. He might be fine preaching in front of 5,000 or leading worship, but asking a beautiful woman out on a date? Now, *that's* challenging!

- It's OK to ask that guy who is a good friend of yours out on a date. It may seem a bit weird on the first date but press through and see what happens.

I remember a young woman who spent lots of time with a great guy called John. When she told me she was fed up with the lack of men around, I said, 'What about John, the guy you spend lots of time with?' After a long discussion she agreed to ask him on a date. But when she asked him the following weekend, he turned her down. She ran round to my house and sat at the kitchen table, saying how terrible it was and how she knew it was a bad idea all along. I prayed with her, gave her coffee and chocolate and was encouraging about the fact that she had tried. A few days later she rang me with lots of excitement in her voice. John had changed his mind and said, 'Why not? Let's give it a go.' The rest . . . is history. They have now been married ten years and have a little girl. They are such good friends, and that's how it started. It was not a mad passionate look across the campus: it was a slow realisation that they liked to chat and spend time together. Their friendship was a great foundation for the ups and downs of married life.

- If the first date is not amazing, do not think the whole thing is doomed. Press through to number two.
- Don't date endlessly. After about three dates with the same person, it's time for the DTR: define the relationship. It will make you feel a bit vulnerable because it's a risk to say what you feel at this point. If you are not interested, you need to say so, politely and clearly. If you are interested, you need to say so. And the guy has to be free to do the same. Otherwise you will both just become frustrated and disappointed.

The DTR is hugely important. If there is one thing that no woman or man should settle for, it's the ill-defined relationship. This does a lot of harm and not a lot of good. You become 'friends with benefits', which really is not being friends at all. It can become a friendship set aside for the weekly pash'n'dash, the cheeky snog when you feel the need. Or you become the back-up plan, the one where you don't do anything physically but virtually get into bed with one another emotionally. You share each other's lives, finish each other's sentences. It feels good for a while because it feels as though you are together, but it's confusing too. You massage each other's feet. (What is it with Christians and massages? Seriously?) You share vulnerabilities and secrets. And when he goes out with someone else you are devastated, because it was a relationship without a title and you just got dumped. Sort of. Don't become Betty Back-up. Do the DTR.

- Always speak with respect and dignity about the person you dated, however it went and even if you decide you don't want to take it any further. Do not run back to all your girlfriends and say how you didn't like the guy's hair or attitude, etc. It's OK to process with one older, wiser person and share generally how it went with your friends. But don't divulge to your girlfriends any personal stuff that the guy might have shared with you: it's not fair. Besides, he might end up dating and marrying one of those girlfriends one day. Awkward.

- It is OK to have dates with several guys in the same church or community. I know this is shocking, but as long as they are not all at the same time it really is OK. You are just saying you want to get to know someone better and away from the rest of the group.

- You cannot 'bagsie' blokes. You cannot play dibs, or make a reservation on a guy you're interested in. Sometimes we tell our friends we like a guy and it's a coded warning that no one else can like him. We say things like, 'Men come and go but your friends are always there for you' (which is not strictly true when we marry him) and warn each other off. We start competing over who got there first, or competing for the guy's attention as we flirt, bake, dress, laugh at rubbish jokes, all for the chance to win his affections. Just for the record, the man in question might have an opinion of his own too! It's awkward and difficult to like the same man as your friends, but if they are friends you've got to be honest and upfront about it.

MORE DATING IDEAS

Seasons change, and with them your circumstances and surroundings. Amy (no, that's not her name) expected to meet her man in a group setting, on a camp or retreat such as she often attended in her college years. But years later she found herself in a career dominated by women, in an area with small churches full of young families. There were no large group settings in which to meet men. She realised her approach and expectations for meeting a guy were set in a bygone era of her life and would need to change.

So what are you prepared to do to give yourself an opportunity to meet some great men? Some of us resist the question because it feels 'desperate'. Again, we're willing to travel all over town for an outfit, travel across the country for a job, invest in an education, and *for a guy . . .*?

Alongside the praying and fasting for a breakthrough, what are you *doing*? Are you actually looking around you to see who is available and not immediately dismissing them because they are not 'perfect for you'? Everyone is worth a second or third glance, and that includes the men at your church.

Are you joining *high-quality* Christian internet dating sites? Joining an online dating agency does not mean you are a sad lonely person. It means you have decided to be active and engaged in something you really want. The dating agency has really taken the place of the old-fashioned matchmaker in the village. It's just that now it's a global village on the internet. Are you going on mission trips which reflect your passions and dreams? Are you serving at Christian festivals? Why not, and why feel so embarrassed about it? You're more likely to meet that guy who is passionate about the kingdom there than at 1 a.m. in a drunken haze with a cheeky snog at a club.

Are you getting together with friends, arranging a speed-dating evening, a dating dinner for you and your friends? Are you going on holiday with lots of other similar-aged people, perhaps joining in an activity such as skiing?[3]

Our favourite example of someone actively pursuing marriage and taking the frontier is where one woman combined her imagination with an entrepreneurial attitude. This woman gathered all her friends one evening and said to them: 'I will give £2,000 to the person from this group who introduces me to my husband.' The result was that her friends were now highly motivated to start arranging dates for her and introducing her to all the eligible males they knew! It also meant she handed over £2,000 to one friend at her wedding a year later. Now that's what we call taking a frontier with all your resources and not just praying and being passive!

If you really want to be married, you have to pursue it.

So what do you think? These are our suggestions, but it's your life. How you move forward with it is up to you. If you are ready to take some practical steps, get together with some girlfriends and begin to pray, brainstorm and *make some practical plans* and be accountable. See what begins to unfold – and enjoy yourself along the way!

9
Conversations over coffee

Sally: I met him when I was just 15. I'd been dancing and skipping and singing my way through childhood; he had been travelling and thinking and talking his way to becoming a teenager. He entered my world through an old rough wooden church door. I walked towards him smiling, wearing blue jeans and clogs with my hair black and curling as ever – slightly wild and unpredictable. He bent slightly to get through the door, leaving his motorbike outside, but bringing his smile inside with him. Someone new . . .

That summer we wound our way through each other's lives: the same church, the same faith, the same friends, the same parties. All to the same soundtrack of Pink Floyd, Tubular Bells, 10cc and Eric Clapton. He became my best friend. He still is.

Jo: It was just a date. A harmless date, a very ordinary date, and then I would get back to my life. I was 28 years old. Enjoying my job, travelling, making plans to buy my first home, enjoying my friends. My housemate and I had been talking about whether we'd adopt children one day. What matters more – that children have two parents or that they are raised in a loving home? And now rather inconveniently this request, invitation, that I had no control over. But I'd promised Sally that I would

be more open, that I would be more proactive. I'd agreed to her chal-
lenge that I should go out with the next guy who asked me on a date, no
matter what. In all honesty, it was an easy challenge to agree to: it never
happened. Until a mission trip to Germany with a team from our church,
where I made some new friends. One of them was an engineer, blond,
five years younger, funny. We laughed all week and promised to hang
out when we got home. So it wasn't a surprise when he got in touch, but
I was completely surprised by what he had to say.

'What's the worst that can happen?' he said. 'Look, if it doesn't work
out it'll be awkward between us for a month and then it'll be normal
again. After all, it's just a date.'

It was just a date, he said.

Whoever thought that a simple conversation could change the trajectory of our lives? The stories above illustrate simple conversations with the men who would be our husbands, but life-changing conversations happen all the time. The words spoken by a friend that help mould our lives. The sermon you heard that seemed to be preached specifically to you. The doctor who tells you 'It's a girl' or 'It's a boy.' The child who splutters 'Mummy'. The conversation with a parent, where you realise that they are simply human beings too and you're an adult now. It seems that good old ordinary life is rather extraordinary after all.

How we are doing relationally includes how we continue in all of our relationships, way beyond the first date, the first kiss, the big day and the first night. We're asking how life is for a couple when the excitement has died down and no one is watching. We're thinking again about friends and family when life has a new label like 'married'. We're considering first thoughts, feelings and fears when you become a parent, and how it changes you.

Marriage, parenting, family – these are huge topics, all deserving much more than a few chapters. Thankfully there are many fantastic books, courses and resources that are available in our local churches and further afield that give a fuller, broader perspective on these stages of life. Whether you're simply being intentional about investing in your relationship or have identified a need for extra support in these areas, make the investment and explore what is out there.

In this chapter we're aiming at something slightly different and hopefully complementary to the resources that are available. We've found that there's a practical kind of wisdom received in intimate conversation with a few girlfriends over a coffee about how life, love and relationships actually work. In their own way these conversations offer the chance to learn, grow and discover what God might be saying to you. They act as examples that have been tested and shaped in the hearts, minds and lives of real women as they walk with God.

So this chapter is an invitation to ponder on a few of our reflections and stories and eavesdrop on a few honest simple conversations about the ongoing journey of relationships. We'll consider how our expectations of married life can differ greatly from reality. We'll look at a few nuts and bolts. Most conversations are between Sally and me, but from time to time you'll hear from our friends. All of them were spoken woman to woman. About marriage, kids, family. Some conversations you'll take particular interest in because they speak to your current phase of life. For others the conversations will purely offer some insights from someone further along in life. Yet those insights about the future might just speak into some of your current decisions. For example, when you catch a glimpse of what marriage looks like, will you change the kind of man you are looking for? This is your chance to eavesdrop. Grab your coffee, sit at a table nearby and discreetly listen in. And periodically we'll turn directly to you and leave you with some reflections and some questions to think about.

MARRIAGE – NOT QUITE WHAT YOU EXPECT . . .

Sally: *I remember watching you standing in my house in an elegant wedding dress, the kind of dress you wondered if you'd ever wear. Years later, what's been the biggest surprise about marriage?*

Jo: *I think there were quite a few surprises. I think one of the first things was realising that I didn't have to be so independent any more. I'd spent my teens making choices for my independence. I'd spent my twenties learning not to put my life on hold, learning to fully embrace and celebrate with the moment I was in regardless of my marital status. Now there was someone who was always there. We're both naturally independent so having this person who was in the house all the time was a bit odd for us both at first. We used to find separate parts of the house for a while, just to read! But strange though it was, it was also incredibly liberating to relax into this relationship where we faced life together.*

The other surprise is that the vast majority of things that I thought mattered when I was single about what kind of guy to marry really don't matter at all – hair colour, age, height, taste in music. Absolutely pointless. And I find myself thanking God because I continually see great qualities in this man that I love that I didn't really look for in a guy back then. Chris works hard, is kind, is open to God stretching him and growing him. He's a strong man who wanted a strong woman. He's so many other things that I learn as we go through life together. Something will happen, a challenge or an opportunity, and he responds in such a way that I think, 'There is no one else I'd want to go through life with. I don't know where we'll end up, but I'm glad I'll be with you.'

Sally: *After over thirty years with Mike, these are some things that have continued through the years. He loves me the same, he still has the ability both to make me laugh and to confront my fears. But life is so very different from when we began, and it's not at all in the place where I expected it to be in so many ways. Even in terms of where we live – Mike and I have always lived in cities, and we love the pace and energy of urban environments. Yet here we are living in the USA in a coastal town of 15,000 people.*

Jo: *So with thirty years (and counting!) behind you, and the hundreds of couples you've discipled over the years, what are some of the observations you've made that you often share with people?*

Sally: *I say to people: if you want to get married, be married, stay married then you both need courage! Marriage takes courage and humility to let go of your own life and way, to die to yourself, so that something new, this shared life, is born. I often talk about expectations within marriage. Quite naturally we all start out with some expectations of what married life 'should' look like, gleaned from our family backgrounds, our communities, conversations with girlfriends, our personal desires. Yet everyone is different, so every marriage is different. Every year in every marriage is different.*

Marriage is all about change! You're both changing with life's differing seasons. So you learn to take your partner with you as you change, and let him in on the bits about you that have altered. You let him in on new dreams, new hopes, on the disappointments and fears. It's about changing together and towards each other and looking towards God. Looking out on the same landscape of life and seeing different things but still choosing to share the view.

SNAPSHOTS OF THE VIEW

Snapshot 1: Julie

Julie met James at church, while he was serving there on a gap year after uni. Julie was 26 when they married and they've been together now for about ten years.

Jo: *When you were single you may have had opinions/expectations about what was important when it came to meeting Mr Right (age, height, calling, etc.). Now that you are married, what have you found is actually important?*

Julie: *James was the first guy I went out with properly. Having similar* values is really important – how you do everyday life together. For me and my husband this is based on God's absolute centrality in our lives, and where we want to go with God is very similar. That's not going somewhere geographically, but our internal values and hearts' desires in terms of pursuing God are similar even though some of the outworking is different because of different personalities and giftings.

Jo: What has been the biggest blessing?

Julie: My husband's love for God that constantly wants me to be the person I'm created to be, and he wants to release me into this the best way he can. That's his heart and I know that even when it isn't easy to navigate.

One of the biggest surprises in marriage for me was that men really do like boobs and bottoms a lot! We are so differently wired sexually. I knew this before to some extent, but I've learned that women are mainly emotionally motivated when it comes to sex.

Another thing is that there are so many constant choices to love and to grow in love, and it won't happen unless you decide to put plans in place to invest in your relationship, and do it!

Jo: What has been the hardest thing?

Julie: Our sex life is a lot harder than I thought it would be and needs to be worked on and consistently committed to, especially on my side.

Jo: How often do you spend time with your female friends?

Julie: I see one friend around once a fortnight for accountability, which is priceless. And I do see other female friends in the week, but it is often with the children so quality conversation doesn't always happen. It's spontaneous time I miss, but I am putting in more girl evening time, although it probably only ends up being once a month.

Jo: If you could give one piece of advice to a newly married woman, what would it be?

Julie: Only one? I could go on and on! OK, so my reflection would be: the more you know how much God loves you and you love yourself, the more love you can bring to the marriage. These things – knowing God's love and getting secure in that – are worth regularly investing in.

Jo: What is your hope for the future?

Julie: *To live in God's love more, to see people's lives transformed through God's love and kingdom breaking out, and for that to be expressed individually, as a couple and as a family, wherever, whenever!*

Snapshot 2: Rowan

Rowan met Matt at university and they married just after her twenty-second birthday. They've been married for about ten years.

Jo: *When you were single you may have had opinions/expectations about what was important when it came to meeting Mr Right (age, height, calling, etc.). Now that you are married, what have you found is actually important?*

Rowan: *The most important thing I have found in looking for a spouse is where he stands with Christ. As long as we have our faith, walk in the same direction and keep Christ as our focus, a lot of the other things in life seem to gain a healthier perspective.*

The biggest surprise about being married is that even after ten years we still have to actively work on our marriage. I guess I thought the more we found out about each other and how we worked, the easier it would be. And while we do know each other better after ten years, we also take a lot of things for granted – I know I catch myself not listening to the ends of sentences because I know what the 'usual' answer has been.

The biggest blessing has been to have a best friend to share all of life with. There have been many moves, cultures, family secrets revealed, relationships, ups and downs, and children, but he has been there through it all.

Jo: *What has been the hardest thing?*

Rowan: *The hardest thing so far in our years together has been to face the prospect of divorce and realise the decision to work on us and stay together was not only in my hands. If we were going to get through a particularly painful chapter of our lives, we would both have to choose to fight for our marriage. When I think of past relationships, I wish I'd protected my heart better than I did. Before I met Matt, I was sure I had* *found the man I would marry, and for the first time I told that other person I loved him. I wish I'd kept those words more sacred than I did. I'm reminded of the Scriptures that talk about 'above all else, guard your heart' and 'do not arouse or awaken love until it so desires'.*

I also wish I hadn't been as physical with past relationships as I chose to be. That, to this day, affects my marriage.

Jo: *How often do you spend time with your female friends?*

Rowan: *Before we moved recently, I made it a priority to meet my girlfriends on a weekly basis. There were about eight of us who became really close. In addition to that I would try to schedule play dates with a few of my closest friends and their kids. Girlfriends, in some ways, can just understand things that a spouse can never understand. It helps to keep me grounded and sane. It also helps to remind me that females are totally different creatures from males.*

Jo: *If you could give one piece of advice to a newly married woman, what would it be?*

Rowan: *You are both on a journey together. However, you will each experience this journey in different, unique ways. This does not make your experience any less important. So speak up, let your voice be heard because your experience and marriage will be stronger for communicating with your spouse what you feel, see, think, question, wonder, need, want, etc.*

Jo: *What is your hope for the future?*

Rowan: *My hope for the future is to find a wiser, more experienced couple whom we can look to for encouragement and wisdom, while we also encourage a younger couple in lessons we have already learned. So that we can model to our children what a healthy relationship with healthy communication looks like.*

Q. What things stand out for you in Julie and Rowan's stories and why? What steps will you take to explore things further?

Jo: *I love Julie and Rowan's honesty about what marriage really looks like and the factors and history that have shaped their marriages. Not* surprisingly, one of the things we might struggle to talk about is the sexual side of the relationship. It's not the thing people want to talk about, but we really need to. But before we talk about sex in marriage, I think it's worth backtracking a little to the dating era and talking about the physical side of a relationship, or sexual experiences of the pash'n'dash variety. When I was growing up there seemed to be this strange contradiction about sex. You weren't supposed to do it because it was wrong and bad and couldn't be undone, but when you were married it was *amazing* and the spiritual thing was to do it as often as possible! I couldn't help but feel that somehow it wasn't simply the ring that made sex good and that people were just trying to scaremonger me into celibacy. As I grew older, I noticed that sometimes women who'd had sex before somehow felt like damaged goods, wondering if any man could want them because they couldn't give their husband their virginity (I'm not sure if the guys who'd slept with them felt the same about themselves). Others just had this creeping feeling that they'd gone too far. There was a lot of condemnation around. Rowan is not the only woman I know who felt her dating life cast a shadow over her sex life when she got married, leaving her with regret. A number of women were sexually active in their younger years, or before they became Christians. Here in the US research indicates that four out of five unmarried evangelicals aged 18–29 have had sex,[1] and I'm sure the numbers in the UK are also higher than we'd care to admit. So it's all a bit complicated. What advice do you give to women in relationships about the physical side of things?

Sally: *One really good method of checking if you are in a good place with the way things are progressing is to make sure that the physical side is staying at the same depth and intimacy level as the emotional and spiritual. They must all move at the same pace. If you are moving towards marriage and this has been fully discussed by both of you then it is reasonable to assume that these three areas will be progressing towards full sexual union after the wedding. Marriage is the context God has designed where a man and a woman becomes 'one flesh'. This is clearly the best option as it is within the security of marriage that full sexual unity can be* *properly enjoyed, along with full emotional openness and full spiritual connection. If you are just dating and have only known the person a little while, it is wise to refrain from fully surrendering yourself to the other completely in each of these three areas, as if the relationship ends you will find yourself grieving its loss to a much greater extent and having to suffer much more. What would you add, Jo? What kind of practical tips do you share when you are mentoring?*

Jo: *I think we have to embrace the reality that celibacy is hard work, and in today's world appears, and frankly feels, rather unrealistic. Theologian Scot McKnight says, 'It's absolutely not realistic, but it's also not realistic not to do a lot of things, and that doesn't mean the Bible doesn't tell us that the ideal and design of God is to not have premarital sex.'² It's a challenge and radically counter-cultural to see sex as a gift for marriage instead of an inevitable consequence and right of expressing your love for someone. It's alien to think that God should have a say, but if our lives are surrendered to Him that includes our sex lives. It's hard, though. It's tough when you've been single for years and fall in love; celibacy's so much easier when a man isn't head over heels in love with you, committed to you, kissing you and telling you how much he loves you. That kind of thing can make you want to undo all the commitments you made to God! And again, since your sex drive is not a wedding gift but resident within, you have to find ways to work it out. It means honest conversations with each other, working out boundaries and, as the Scriptures say, fleeing temptation! I mean, get up and leave if needed. You might need to be aware of your monthly cycle and when you are likely to be most turned on, times of the day when you are most likely to ignore the decisions you've made. And someone to be accountable to, I found, was a great passion-killer! That's why I talked to you about it back in the day, more than my peers. My premarital sex life was the conversation I never really wanted to have with you, so it helped me make sure I didn't.*

I think, on a practical level, that the length of our relationships today makes it harder. We fall in love and go out together for two or three years, then are engaged for ever. In the culture of the Bible marriage was arranged and people were often younger. Again, it's McKnight who says that we need to wrestle through the implications of that for young adults who are waiting for much, much longer.

Sally: *Mike and I always recommend short engagements, because when you've made that decision, you really need to just get on with it!*

Jo: *I totally agree! By that point of your relationship you are crazy in love, you can't be bothered to go home at night because you want to be together 24/7. And when we looked into each other's eyes, it was as if in my head all I could hear was Marvin Gaye's 'Let's Get It On'! Not helpful! Sometimes the answer to this is get married. Soon.*

Sally: *The other thing I always, always want my girls I disciple to know, though, is that we have a Redeemer who has carried our past and can and does transform our lives.*

Jo: *Absolutely – none of this 'damaged goods' lie that seems to beset some of us. Some women have had sex and regretted it, some have had sex and frankly didn't. And some women are unhappy about how far their relationships sometimes went physically before they married. It's important to know that God forgives, restores, redeems.*

Depending on the situation, consider talking and praying the situation through with your accountability partner, a mentor, a prayer minister. For some of us this goes beyond our sexual history. We may have had horrendous sexual experiences, abuse, rape. He is your Redeemer too. Yes, prayer is essential, but we would also urge you to talk to a Christian trained professional to help you process what has happened to you and help you discover the tools to move forward in your relationships with men.

Jo: *So what about sex when you are married? Any hot tips? One of the best pieces of advice given by a friend was that after they were married, on their wedding night, the first thing they did was pray and dedicate* *their sex life to God. I think it's a great idea. I think it's also good to be really practical, and say in general this is an area of life where lots of practice really helps! Your thoughts?*

Sally: *I like to remind women that sex doesn't stand alone in your relationship; many things affect this area of your married life:*

1 Hormones, your time of the month. Sometimes you're not interested. Sometimes you are very interested.

2 If you have had major conflict of any kind with anyone, but especially your spouse, often you don't feel very sexy until it's resolved.

3 Fears. It makes a difference if you are struggling with or battling some fear or insecurity.

4 Tablets. Sometimes a prescription drug affects your libido.

5 Pregnancy! Interestingly this can go either way, but it has an effect!

6 Illness. It can be chronic pain or just a cold, but it usually means a woman is not that bothered.

7 A big project, e.g. moving house. If it takes up your emotional energy it can take away from your interest in sex.

8 A big career change can mean big sexual appetite change.

9 Drink. If you only have sex when you are under the influence you may want to ask yourself why.

10 Place. If you are away from home, e.g. at friends', on retreat, at your parents' house. These places can also affect your mood for sex.

I encourage women to think this one through and talk with their husband so he knows where they're coming from. However, I also explain to them that their men will generally see things differently! Basically, nothing usually stops a healthy young male's appetite for sex. Not flu, not a caravan, nor major building work going on two feet from your bedroom window!

Jo: *OK, less talk about making babies. What about having babies?*

Sally: *Getting married was not a big deal to me compared to this. Having a baby, a small living breathing dependent human being who was totally relying on me to not screw it up, was scary. Nothing has made me look at God's identity and character and face my identity and character like having children. They're in their twenties now and I'm still discovering!*

Jo: *I wholeheartedly agree! I'd always wanted children, always expected to have them, and was pretty resolved that whether I'd give birth to my own or adopt, children were a part of my future. But when Chris mentioned that he'd like to start trying for a family, you'll remember how freaked out I was and how we needed to take one of our long drives to somewhere anonymous so I could get my head around the idea.*

Sally: *I remember it well. It took a while to talk you down!*

Jo: *I think I was confronted with so many thoughts and fears. On one level, it was realising that life wouldn't be the same again. I knew that motherhood would change me, not just physically but emotionally and spiritually too. There was a moment when I knew I'd even have to look at my past differently. It was one thing dealing with my own junk but, as you say, passing it on to someone else was another thing entirely. I wondered if I was up to the task, if I would be good enough as a mum. I knew I'd love my kids, but would I love them enough? This was not an area in life that I wanted to get wrong. Years later, I'm pretty philosophical about how I felt then. Now I know that God is with us, helping us bring up our children, that there's more room in my heart for kids than I thought possible. Now I know that I make mistakes, I learn and grow, and I've discovered again that His power really is made perfect in my weakness. But back then, all I had was a lot of fear and a vivid imagination – a toxic combination. Chris never pressured me, but he gently raised the issue from time to time, encouraging me to face what was going on inside. He was calm, clear and confident; he could see something that I couldn't. I began to wonder if it was time to submit, let go*

137

in some way and start working things through. Which led me to that conversation in the car with you . . .

Sally and I can talk about these kinds of things for ever; we often do, for hours. But we've noticed that our eavesdroppers, the women we journey with, seem a little uncomfortable. It's not that they are not interested, it's just that they have a question, a burning question that they want to ask. More than that, it's a question that they want to hear our answers to, theologically and practically. And they don't care if it's in a conversation or a chapter. The question begins as a murmur, but soon it's loud and clear. **What about submission? How do you work all of that out?**

10

Standing eyeball to eyeball

WELL, WHAT ABOUT SUBMISSION?

> Submit to one another out of reverence for Christ. Wives, submit
> yourselves to your own husbands as you do to the Lord. For the
> husband is the head of the wife as Christ is the head of the church,
> his body, of which he is the Saviour. Now as the church submits to
> Christ, so also wives should submit to their husbands in everything.
> Husbands, love your wives, just as Christ loved the church and gave
> himself up for her.
>
> (Eph. 5:21–25)

This is one of the most pressing questions we've come across when
we talk about women standing 'eyeball to eyeball' with their men.
How do you stand eyeball to eyeball with your man if really he is
in charge and you are supposed to submit to him? And what does
that *mean,* anyway? Many of us really wrestle with God and with
the Church (not the same thing) on this, frustrated, confused and
feeling that for all the liberating talk about a Saviour who sets us
free, we've just been shackled when we weren't looking! We're
worried that submission requires that we disengage our brains and

say yes to everything that we're told, obedience without question, like compliant children. If he wants sex, then you have to agree, enthusiastically! If he wants to spend all your money, you have to go along with it. You wear what he tells you to wear. And even when he's wrong he's right, because he's the head and your job is to obey. Your husband knows better than you, God said so. Women are asking questions about whether they're allowed to have an opinion within their own marriage, whether the insights, gifts and skills that are deployed in our careers and are part of the fabric of our other relationships have any place within our marriage.

Once Sally and I were talking to a group of young leaders, many of whom were married couples. As she shared her story, Sally told the group that when she and Mike were called to a new place, she normally had the sense that God was up to something before Mike did. It wasn't intended to be a major part of her story, it was just a fleeting comment. Yet when it was time for Q and A, one of the young married women asked her to unpack that moment a bit more. 'Do you mean that you sometimes get the guidance first, that God tells you what the family will be doing next, if it's time to move on?' Sally replied, 'Yes, it happens a lot of the time. Mike is a very strong character, a strong leader, but it just happens that I tend to get the sense of God prodding us in a new direction earlier than Mike does.' Soon a number of the wives in the room were asking similar questions. We realised that some of the group were surprised to think that God would speak to Sally before her husband and that this could be OK. They wondered if it was the man's role to get the sense of direction and calling first, whether it spoke of his position in the family.

So what do women's and men's roles look like and what does submission mean? Again, volumes have been written on this topic alone, so we can't possibly do the topic justice in a few paragraphs and at the back of this book we'll suggest some books and articles for wider reading. But we don't want to avoid it either. In the meantime, we're going to present a few thoughts for you to consider, argue with (obviously you don't have to agree!) and use as a springboard for your own research.

First, it's important to note that these verses from Ephesians, and similar ones describing submission (see Colossians 3:18–19 and 1 Peter 3:5–6), are unpacked specifically in the context of marriage, not in relation to how women are supposed to relate to men in general, as has been assumed by some Christians. Both the Ephesians and Colossians passages are written by Paul, who had at least one married couple on his team where the woman was known to play a more prominent role (Priscilla) and who was very vocal in his support of women in leadership in a culture which barely saw their value (Rom. 16). He said to the Galatian church, 'There is neither Jew nor Gentile, neither slave nor free, nor is there male and female, for you are all one in Christ Jesus' (Gal. 3:28). Contrary to what many people think, Paul was very pro women. Yet what did he have to say about women when it came to marriage?

MARRIAGE IN PAUL'S WORLD

A closer look at the context of the Graeco-Roman world to which Paul writes gives us greater insights. In Paul's world, everyone's role in society was defined by a 'household code'. The man had complete control of the household by law. His rule was absolute, and no one in the household (his wife, his children, his slaves) could legally challenge this. As David Hamilton notes, 'Submission was a one way street from wife to husband, from child to father, and from slave to master.'[1]

The purpose of marriage was largely about producing children and thus preserving the family line. The inability to produce children, especially sons, could often be grounds for a man to divorce his wife. The average age of the husband upon marriage was 30, while the woman would be less than 18. This was a world where women were not greatly valued, where a man might enjoy the company of his prostitute rather than his wife to satisfy both his sexual and his intellectual needs. Theologian Gordon Fee notes: 'In this kind of household, the idea that men and women might be equal partners in marriage simply did not exist.'[2]

How does Paul speak to the infant church in this world, where this pattern of life was not only accepted but seen as the fabric of society?

It's worth exploring where Paul's perspective on submission begins. We often start the conversation in Ephesians 5 verse 22 with 'wives'. Perhaps some of our Bibles even have a subtitle introducing a new section of Paul's thought there. It's important to remember that those subtitles are not in the original text: they were added later by translators and editors with a rather daunting job on their hands, and are generally a great help in separating the flow of what is said. Paul has been writing to the Ephesian community about the Christian lifestyle. No matter who or what they were before, following Jesus would change how they conducted their everyday lives. If they had been thieves, it was time to get a job and become generous (Eph. 4:28). If they had been promiscuous, that would need to change (Eph. 5:3). They were called to live wisely (5:15). It was a high calling, and Paul knew they couldn't do it in their own strength. So he instructed them to walk away from drunkenness and its seemingly inevitable consequences, and to be filled and go on being filled with the Holy Spirit. What would a Spirit-filled life look like? Instead of trash talk (4:29), they would speak differently, proclaiming God's Word over one another. They would have an attitude of gratitude that would overflow from a thankful heart. But evidence of the Spirit was not just found in the way they spoke or sang, but also in how the Ephesian community, men and women, related to one another. Out of their devotion and love for their Saviour, the body of Christ would be marked by relationships of *mutual submission* one to another. 'According to the text, where there is no mutual submission, reverence for Christ is wanting.'[3] Life in the Spirit transformed the household code, starting with marriage itself.

And so it's in verse 21 that we actually find the word 'submit'. It's in the context of mutual submission within the wider Christian community that we learn what life in the Spirit means for married life, for both men and women. In the original Greek the word 'submit' isn't in verse 22 – the modern translations include it because of the use of the ellipsis in Greek pointing to what verse 22 means – but because of the sentence structure it's clear that submission in marriage is what Paul is about to explore next. 'Submit to one another out of reverence for Christ . . . Wives . . . to your own husbands as you do to the Lord.'[4]

If submission means simply to obey without question because we are somehow less significant or important, what would that mean for the wider Christian community that Paul instructs to 'submit to one another'? How would that work practically in daily life if people had opposing views in a situation and they had to automatically obey one another? It's important that we take a step away from what we are afraid or frustrated that submission might mean, and look again at the word itself.

The Greek word translated 'submit' is *hypotasso*. *Hypotasso* comes from two words, *hupo*, meaning 'next after' or 'under', and *tasso*, meaning 'arrange after' or 'arrange under'. In a military context it referred to arranging soldiers in files, or under the command of their leader.[5] In non-military usage it can mean to show respect and courtesy, to unite one person with another, to remain in another's sphere of influence.[6]

Katherine Bushnell contends, 'The true sense of the word describes the Christian grace of yielding one's preferences to another, where principle is not involved, rather than asserting one's rights.'[7] Michele Guinness further notes that submission challenges our need for control within our relationships: 'It urges us to let go, give way, and value our partner's opinion as much as our own.'[8]

Submission doesn't mean I have no thoughts or opinions. It certainly doesn't suggest I'm of less value in the world, in my husband's eyes or in God's eyes. It doesn't mean I don't ask questions, address problems or need to stay silent on things that I believe are important. But it does mean I'm not at the centre of my universe and life and marriage, that life doesn't happen on my terms. It does mean that I am not in control of everything that happens in our marriage. When we are looking at our lives, our money, our children, our calling, submission means I let go of my passionately held views and am open to take on my husband's perspective. On one level this really isn't that radical: it's a marriage, not a competition or some twisted battle for dominance. Why would I marry a man who I was afraid – or even knew – would control my every move, who would need to extinguish my views in order to have his own? Who would ignore my every thought and opinion, who would have no respect for the things I cared about? Isn't that what we're most afraid of? But what kind of relationship would that be? And as for yielding to his perspective, why would I commit my life to a man whose opinions I couldn't trust, whose views I had no respect for anyway?

So yes, submission means that we are prepared to yield our way, our terms, in the relationship. It means we show respect and courtesy, that we embrace our loved one's influence in our lives, and unite with him. And in letting go, that will inevitably mean sometimes doing what our spouse prefers instead of what we prefer. Sometimes, submission is easy; sometimes, not so much. No wonder Paul unpacks this in the context of a life lived in the power of the Holy Spirit!

Yet it's not as alien as it sounds when you consider the relationships in your life. We all naturally see nothing wrong with living life our way. It's in relationship with others that we come undone.

We need the Spirit to guide us to live differently, to be different. Life with God means that we all, men and women, live in mutual submission. There'll be many occasions when we've submitted to another's point of view, or desires, because no one ever gets life all their own way.

Imagine a group of friends who all want to have a girls' getaway, the holiday to beat all holidays. You've worked hard for it, you know you need it and you want to be together. There's only one problem: you want to go to different places. Two of you want to go to Greece, having always wanted to spend some time sunning yourselves on a beach with a cool beverage on the island of Zante. But the other two are more drawn to a shopping trip to New York, taking in the sights and sounds of the Big Apple, catching a show on Broadway, laughing all the way. Both ideas sound fabulous, but they are very different and you clearly can't do both. Everyone has a valid reason for the trip of their choice. So what do you do? You could split into two groups, but the point of this girls' getaway is that you go together. The only way it will work is if someone chooses to let go, to submit for the sake of the bigger vision of enjoying a fabulous holiday with your favourite girls. Team NYC, could you submit to Team Zante? What about you, Team Zante? Are you ready to let go?

Q. Pause for thought: what do *you* think submission in marriage looks like?

AND WHAT ABOUT HEADSHIP?

For the husband is the head of the wife as Christ is the head of the church, his body, of which he is the Saviour.
(Eph. 5:23)

> But I want you to realise that the head of every man is Christ, and the head of the woman is man, and the head of Christ is God.
>
> (1 Cor. 11:3)

Again, these lines have perplexed many of us. How does this make sense if we are called to submit to one another? The word *kephale*, translated 'head' (also used in 1 Corinthians 11 in reference to marriage) has been interpreted in a number of ways. For some, 'head' means boss, the person in charge. But many scholars note that a legitimate interpretation of the word 'head' is 'source' or 'origin', so that the husband is the source or origin of the wife (think ribs and creation), in the same way that Christ is the source or origin of the Church (Eph. 5:23) and, in relation to the Corinthians passage, in the same way that God is the source of Jesus Christ.

Whatever our perspective, of even more significance is the nature of headship. We so easily read words like 'head' and infuse them with twenty-first-century cultural (often secular) interpretations and expressions of leadership, and understandably freak out. The head becomes the autocratic CEO, the dictator. Our understanding is that these types of leaders are loud, bold, dynamic personalities who make all the decisions and control everything. Nothing can be questioned if you want to keep your position and not be deemed rebellious. In this culture, to speak out is to undermine the leader. It seems as though we've reverted back to the Graeco-Roman household code, and the best we can hope for is a benevolent version. But how did Jesus, the head of the Church, relate to others? Are these the leadership qualities He demonstrated in His ministry? We certainly see times where Jesus challenged and spoke very boldly, and where He even overturned tables and drove out money-changers in the temple. But that was in response to the religious leaders who stood in the way of real faith, or demonic powers that kept people captive. There were definitely occasions when Jesus said some challenging words to the disciples, and times when He was directive. But when it came to leadership, Jesus told His disciples very clearly that they were to lead in a very different way from what they saw in the world around them. They were not to lord it over the people around them: they were to be servants, to go last, to humble themselves, as in fact He had (Luke 22:24–27).

Q. Pause for thought: what could it mean for a husband to be a servant?

Paul encourages husbands to love their wives as Christ loved the Church, which, knowing the cultural context, was radical enough. But again perhaps we have modernised the word 'love' here and made it purely romantic. We look at it and think it simply means tenderness, date nights, loving actions, kindness. While we don't want to negate any of those wonderful things (which frankly we'd hope would be integral to any marriage), we maintain that Paul is pushing for something even richer and more expansive than that. The word for 'love' here is not *eros*, which refers to romantic love, nor *phileo*, which references friendship; it's *agape*. *Agape* is the way in which Jesus loved people: a sacrificial love, which motivated Jesus to lay down His life for others. So when Paul calls for the man of the house – whose word is law, who could divorce a woman for not bearing a child – to sacrificially love his wife, his world has just been turned upside down.

CHRISTIANS, RAISE YOUR GAME!

So with all this in mind, what is Paul trying to get across?

Paul stands boldly and calls believers to raise their game and the understanding of marriage. Rather than existing solely to provide descendants, it's now a metaphor of Christ and the Church. We remember that the early church met in people's homes, not in buildings with stained-glass windows or multipurpose buildings with high-quality sound systems. There were no cathedrals built to illustrate the might and power of God. These were the days when church really did mean the people – neither the institution, nor a building. Alongside that, the home in Paul's time was not purely a private place of retreat from the daily grind of the world, as it's often viewed today. It also functioned as the public place of business, commerce and creativity, depending on the household trade. While the man of the house and his highest-ranking slaves had a more public role, the wife's world was often limited to the private functions of the home. Paul's challenge to the conventions of the day meant that people, lost and saved, would see who Christ was, how He lived and loved, not just through words and deeds but through transformed relationships within the household. What an incredible witness! This was beyond radical: it was revolutionary. It would require nothing less than a complete paradigm shift in men's and women's attitude and approach to the institution of marriage. Marriage would now be a conduit of God's grace and mercy, an illustration of covenant relationship and kingdom values. Continually filled with the Spirit, it would illustrate and embody the servanthood and the sacrificial love of Jesus. It would illustrate how God's people would respond to such sacrificial love, in submitted relationships, liberated from fear, competition and control. And thus Christian marriage would stand a world apart from marriages within the limitations of the prevailing culture. You can't fake healthy, whole, sacrificially loving relationships. People would know that these Christians were motivated by something, Someone, who transformed them from the inside out. And as the growth of the early church would indicate, the witness of the lives of the first believers proved utterly compelling.

Today's culture has its own limited understanding of marriage. It's easily disposable, often reduced to one expensive day. Enthroned in fantasy and fairytales, many couples begin married life ill-equipped for the challenge and opportunity of two lives coming together as one. In fact, we've been immersed in a culture that encourages, even exalts, individualism and independence. 'Sacrifice', 'servanthood' and 'submission' seem like archaic, oppressive words, where we lose who we are and miss out. These words are reduced to who gets to be in charge, who is allowed to do what, go first, make decisions, as though marriage were designed to be competing voices fighting for supremacy. It's no wonder we approach marriage tentatively, fearful of the life-draining restrictions it might bring. Yet real sacrifice and submission look very different . . .

Sally: When Mike and I were about 27 years old we were looking for a church to give our time, talent and energies to. Mike had already done four years out of theological college in two places in Cambridge, and now we had two beautiful precious little girls; where we chose to go would affect them now as well.

We had many suggestions, many of which I would have liked to have gone to. But one day we got a letter about a parish in London, Brixton Hill: it was a small inner-city place that had just recovered from the 1982 riots. We looked at the letter and decided to go and see it.

We travelled from the beautiful spires of Cambridge to the litter-filled pavements of Brixton. We looked around and all I could see was terrible poverty and tragic people living desperate lives. I hated it – instantly. I did not want my sweet little girls to grow up among the filth and destruction that I saw everywhere in this place. I did not want to live in the vicarage that was pressed in behind the church and had broken doors and cracked windows. I did not want to shop in the local stores that smelt strange and had bars on the doors.

So we came to the end of the day and drove to discuss it somewhere on the Streatham High Road. We sat face to face in a booth; I was pushing pizza around on my plate while tears dripped on to my napkin. I hated it, but I knew Mike had a vision for the place. He could see himself here. He could imagine how he could bring the gospel to this horrible place, but he would not come alone: he would bring me and our two girls with him. He also knew I didn't want to go.

*He then did something that set the tone for the rest of our life in ministry together. He waited. He said, 'I know you don't want to come here and **I won't make you.** But I want you to do one thing for me. Pray over the next three days, and tell me at the end of that time what God has said to you about it. **Whatever He says we will do.** But we won't discuss it till the end of the third day.'*

This was one of the wisest things he has ever done.

He waited for me, and he trusted me. What a gift. So, in submission, I did what he asked. I prayed and prayed amid the havoc of daily life with toddlers, and I waited for revelation. I did get revelation, and it was clear: three promises, three Scriptures, three pictures – to go to Brixton. We sat down at the end of the third day, I unloaded all that had been going on in my prayer life, and we decided to go.

In the end we were there for four years, but in my heart I had committed to go for life.

I had submitted to my husband, but he had also loved me the way Jesus loved the Church: sacrificially. The word 'submission' does not mean 'doormat'. It does not mean to have no opinion. I think of submission as being like submitting a paper or an idea and waiting to see what happens. It gives us time to put all our thoughts and feelings down on paper, or verbally to our husband, about the matter at hand. We then walk away, knowing that our husband's part is to love us sacrificially as Jesus does the Church. When a couple are both operating on these principles, sometimes I think the woman gets the easier option.

This is just one example concerning a big life-changing decision, but there are so many others. There are still challenges in Paul's words for twenty-first-century men and women. He challenges us to look at what sacrificial love and submission mean to our desires and choices and rights; what serving looks like in how we relate to one another. Perhaps it's important to explore what it means for two independent people raised in today's culture to become one flesh and live as one in Christ Jesus. What would it look like to act like Jesus in your marriage? If we took the time to find out, would our marriages be transformed, and what would they say to those around us?

EYE TO EYE

So how is a woman *supposed* to act, what is she *supposed* to be like in a marriage? The idea that there is a way women are 'supposed' to be is laden with the potential for putting us in unhelpful boxes, but it's still a question women often ask! Michele Guinness's insight that *ezer* is also a verb, meaning protect, surround, defend and cherish,[9] gives us a great perspective. Every one of these meanings is an important aspect of how we approach married life. They denote strength and tenderness, proactivity, nurture and intimacy. Furthermore, the *ezer knegedu* stands boldly opposite her man: 'In other words, Eve is right in Adam's face, nose to nose, eyeball to eyeball. They can gaze at each other with love and longing, or confront if necessary, and it often is.'[10]

To face each other with both love and challenge is a hard thing to do. We're often ready to comfort or be comforted, but we're not sure how we feel about being confronted and challenged to grow and mature in everyday life. No one enjoys being confronted with the reality of who they truly are, even when it's 'the truth in love'. Who wants to feel as if they've failed? Who wants to be wrong? Who wants to discover that they are selfish? But when we live in such close proximity to someone, we are bound to see each other's less-than-beautiful side. In fact, sometimes living in such close proximity ignites it! But if we want to become more like Christ in our hearts and lives, then we need the opportunity to develop our characters, to work at the things within us that keep us far from Jesus. Married life is one of those great opportunities! Husbands and wives are the first instruments of change in each other. It's not very romantic and it's not in the movies or the fairytales, but it's true.

Sally: I love what we see of Adam and Eve in Genesis 1 and 2, because we see that with God at the centre there's so much potential for our relationships. *But standing eyeball to eyeball isn't always easy. We need to know we are secure enough to see this happen on a regular basis. If we're prepared to challenge our husbands, we have to expect that our husbands will do this back to us! I knew I needed this from my husband. So I married a man who I knew would do this for me with godly insights and with love. We naively believe when we are married that love will be enough. It's never enough. It was enough for me for about two weeks into marriage.*

We started our married life in a cold miserable flat on a horrible housing estate in London nicknamed 'Devil's Island'. We had bits and pieces of furniture and some wedding gifts. We had each other, as the saying goes, but I worked at an estate agent's from 9 a.m. to 5 p.m. and my husband was a youth worker working from 4 p.m. to 12 a.m.! I had no friends, no money, no car, no phone. It was so hard. Real life stared me hard and brutal in the face and it was not what I had expected. I cried every day. Mike would come home at midnight and find me crying into my duvet or into the dishes. I loved him but I hated this place, this life I had chosen.

Did he say, 'It's going to get better'? No. Did he say he could make it better? No. What he did was challenge me to dig deep and rely on God. He said, 'His grace will be sufficient; He is faithful and He will be to you too.' It was a good challenge. The lessons I learned about myself, my selfishness and my needs have lasted me long into my life today. If Mike had sidestepped that moment, that face-to-face challenge, it would have been harder later. Instead he looked at me with all the love of a newly married man in his early twenties and told me he wasn't going to solve it. He knew he couldn't. He gave me a huge gift. I learned, even stand-ing next to the love of my life, that God was my Rock. So many times we look solely to each other to solve our hurts, needs or difficulties. Many times I see young, sweet, tender-hearted men unable to go face to face with their wives in doing this. They do them a severe injustice. They say they feel afraid that the challenge would not be interpreted as love. But it is; it's the mark of true love. I think we need to start by giving our husbands permission to challenge us. To say to them, 'I may cry, stamp, shout or throw dishes during the process of the challenge, but if you stick with me in it and are not afraid I will still love you for this – and possibly even more.' To say to them, 'Thank you for not allowing me to stay where and who I was, but for being with me in this journey of discovery towards where God wants my heart to be.' We need to allow them to be this for us.

Are you ready to stand eyeball to eyeball with your man? Not in some weird competition to have the last word, to control or manip-ulate, but with love and longing to share hard truths when they need to be said? Or will you live in disappointment with your love, resenting him because 'he should just know' what needs to change. Yes, you are his wife, but will you also be his *ezer*? Will you protect, surround, defend and cherish? There are times when wives need to challenge their husbands too. We'll need to stand eye to eye look-ing at them with love and challenging them, not for our sake or for the sake of a tidy house or the errands and chores we want them to do for us, but for their heart's sake and God's glory. We'll need to find ways of doing this for our husbands without nagging or manipulation.

WHEN YOU NEED TO STAND EYE TO EYE:
A PAINFUL EXAMPLE

Sometimes standing eyeball to eyeball will be very challenging when we have to address one another's brokenness. We carry our lives into our marriages, and sometimes that means we bring our addictions and habits that we need to break free of. Rather than being filled with shame and hiding from reality, or colluding with one another's problems, we look at one another and address unhelpful addictive habits. So, for example, suppose your husband has relied on pornography since his teens. He's wanted to stop, but he can't beat this and is ashamed and frustrated with his failure. You've discovered a magazine, seen something alarming in your internet history, and it's breaking your heart. What happens now? Don't pretend the problem doesn't exist in the name of being a supportive spouse. You need to address it and have the challenging conversation. Ask the question. You know, the one that's been forming somewhere in the back of your mind, the question that's been tugging your heart and causing anxiety. Ask it when you have time to hear the answer properly. Once the answer is yes, it's out there. You have the information, and what are you going to do?

This is the point where you have to really press into all of God's grace and resources, asking for the power and strength to walk through the anger, the pain and the hurt. It's where you love the man but not the behaviour. It's a battle, so you need to have a process and to come up with a plan together.

Here's a suggested process:

- Look at what the trigger is for this pattern of behaviour. Is it when he is Hungry, Angry, Lonely or Tired – HALT? Observe the behaviour and the pattern. Don't be afraid: this is no moment for fear. Press on into the battle.
- When, where and how does this habit happen, and how can

you address this? Restrictions added to computers and smart phones may be a start. Maybe you need to move the computer to a more public place, visible to all, rather than keeping it in a cosy private study.

- Look at your wider support network. It's easy to think all you need is each other, and it's tempting because of the vulnerability you feel, but you need your wider community. He needs to be accountable, to you and to some men. Does he have friends he can be accountable with, or a mentor? Does he need to seek out a support group or a counsellor? You'll need support too. Find a friend who can pray and support you, not to husband-bash but to stand with you. You'll have your own things to deal with as a result of this situation. There may be feelings of sexual inadequacy and unattractiveness, of failure and loss, of bitterness and unforgiveness.

- Grief will be an overwhelming feeling that stalks you unexpectedly. It's really OK to shout and cry and rage at God over all of this. He is certainly big enough to take it and *He* will come to your rescue.

- Even after the worst is over, do not dodge the hard questions. Have a regular time when you can ask about how it is all going in your husband's life. Ask directly. Check in with this question every few months and then every year.

Again, this is just one example of a difficult area a couple might face in a chapter of their married life together. We know that pornography is not just a battle for men, and there are lots of addictive habits that can be destructive in our relationships, such as drinking too much, overeating, even overworking. Overworking is very destructive, mainly because it comes in the guise of provision for you and your family. The key principle that we want to stress here is that couples don't have to be paralysed by fear in troubled times. You don't have to feel stuck and hopeless in those moments. We can have those difficult conversations, face those overwhelming circumstances, because we do so knowing that we don't even do marriage in our own strength, but filled continuously with the Holy Spirit. Not only that, we can draw on the resources, support and experience within Christ's Body, the Church, to help us through. If you're in the midst of a difficult patch, consider the process and people you need to surround yourself with to help you through.

And finally . . .

Wherever your marriage is today, keep investing in your relationship! Here are a few suggestions:

- Invest in your relationship with God, both separately and together. You'll love each other better when you love God first. Find time to pray together and for one another, read and talk about Scripture together. Discover what God is doing in each other's lives and encourage and affirm one another. Worship God together and on your own, but as part of a wider worshipping community.
- Put your spouse above your girlfriends, above your family, above your job. Make time for one another, with date nights and getaways. If you have young children and family are nearby, make the most of opportunities to get away and leave the kids to have a great time with the rellies. If your family are far away, build a local extended family, people whom you trust and who love your kids and would be happy to look after them. Pay babysitters well!
- Don't let your lives coexist under the same roof: do things together. It could be that you read the same book together or take up a hobby together, or you serve in your local church or community together.
- Have lots of great sex, and don't worry if it takes some practice!
- If your marriage hits a rough patch, don't be afraid to seek out some help within your church community or a professional

counsellor. Whether you hit a rough patch or not, be aware of marriage retreats and courses that are available at your church or in your region.

- Have friends. You still need them, and not just married ones who are like you!
- Enjoy your life together. Sounds obvious, but rather than always dreaming of what could be, sometimes it's good to stop, take stock of where you are and be thankful.

MOVING ON

It feels as though we could say so much more but we need to keep on moving, because our journey with you is reaching its final stages. We've looked at how you are spiritually and checked our spiritual foundations. We've looked at how you approach a few of your key relationships. From there we need to ask ourselves how we are practically engaging with our lives. Life happens to us every single day, demanding a response. Are you avoiding life, still waiting to be rescued? Or are you ready to engage with the life that you have?

11
Life unexpected . . .

'It's definitely a boy!' the ultrasound technician announced. Chris and I smiled as we looked at the screen, watching the technician point out the relevant parts of our first child. He explained that he liked to be especially thorough, looking for the obvious but also for other indicators such as the baby's heart rate. And so it was with great confidence that he said, 'I've been in this business for twenty years, I know all the signs. You are definitely having a boy.' My firstborn would be a son and we called him Reuben John. Over the next few months we bought lots of blue clothes and toys and decorated a jungle-themed nursery. As our baby grew inside me we talked to him, sang to him, imagined what he'd look like, what sports he would play. We prayed for him passionately and I discovered that though I'd never felt especially broody, I was every inch a mum. Though I had not met him yet, I fiercely loved my child and life would never be the same again.

In the last few weeks of my pregnancy my doctor grew concerned that my blood pressure was rising rather rapidly, so he decided I needed to be induced. For twelve hours I sat waiting for something to happen, and nothing did. So he broke my waters with something that either was or distinctly resembled a rather long knitting needle, and it hit me: suddenly brutal contractions, sweat, pain, weariness. With only ice cubes for food, I rued the unfairness that men don't give birth and demanded why they couldn't give me stronger drugs, like now!

Somewhere in the midst of it all the moment came and my baby was born. The doctor lifted the baby in the air and for a moment there was silence. Well, actually the baby was crying but Chris and I were silent. Something didn't quite add up, but in the euphoria and the blood and sweat and drugs I didn't know what it was. We later learned that in that moment we were thinking exactly the same thing:

'That's a funny-looking boy.'

Chris was waiting for *something to unfold*, while I was just dazed. Then the doctor announced loudly, with surprise in his voice:

'*It's a girl!*'

It's a girl. *Reuben is a girl?* Reuben is *a girl*. A girl.

Chris seemed to look up to the heavens and sigh, both overjoyed at being a daddy and relieved that he need no longer worry about his son's anatomical challenges. I said, 'It's Tia May!', the name we'd originally chosen if our baby was a girl, and I reached out my arms to hold my firstborn. (Both she and her sister Zoë would enter the world defying expectations.) Tia May is definitely a girl. Our friends immediately went shopping and delivered gifts. In pink (and yes, I see the irony here).

ONE PLUS ONE EQUALS . . . ?

Have you noticed the way that life doesn't always turn out the way we anticipate? Regardless of what happens in the world of mathematics, in life things don't always add up. Sometimes, no matter how definite we are, it's a girl. Life ignores our expectations and overlooks our plans. You'll have seen that the issue of expectations is something of a recurring motif in this book, and with that the realisation that we have to lay down some of them as we journey through life with God. There are things we do and don't expect for our lives embedded in our minds and hearts. Our happiness often depends on them.

Sometimes life outside the box is a pleasant surprise of unexpected blessings, financial provision, new friends and relationships. Other times life's unexpected is not welcome. You didn't expect that the relationship would break up and that he'd moved on so quickly and commit to her. He always struggled to commit to you, but he told her he loved her. You didn't expect that that friendship wouldn't last – she'd been such a significant part of your twenties. How was she able to move on without you? You didn't ever think you couldn't have children; you love children, you've always wanted children. Why couldn't it be you? You didn't expect to be wrestling with chronic illness. You didn't expect to sit in that doctor's clinic and feel time stand still as you heard a terrifying diagnosis. You feel too young to have lost a parent; you can't imagine you will never hear their voice again. You thought divorce would never ever happen to you. And yet for all the vows you made and meant, here you are, wondering if your life is over. You didn't expect to bring up your children alone. You thought life would be better, easier, when you left home, when you were independent. You thought your relationships with your parents would improve with time, not get worse! You didn't expect you would be out of work this long. You thought you'd be able to keep the house. You thought, you hoped, you expected . . . something different.

Life is wonderful, and can offer us some wonderful surprises. But it's also heartbreaking at times. No wonder the fairytales are so compelling. We can always expect a happily ever after there, and one in our favour. Life is so much sweeter in our expectations, our dreams. Yet sometimes on the journey, when you are talking about how you are doing spiritually, relationally and practically, your life doesn't fit neatly into a section. All you can do is stop for a while and acknowledge how life actually is, for there are no strategies, no easy answers. Sometimes there are no answers at all. Life happened, and reality left you gasping for breath.

Q. Where have your expectations for your life not been met? How are you dealing with it?

Sally: I'm no expert on grief, but I know I've seen many young women grieve over the loss of their dreams. And once that woman was me.

My life at 27 was not quite what I had expected. I thought I would be married, but probably to a teacher. I would own my own home, with unique, beautiful pieces of furniture Mike and I had collected at weekends. It would have a carefully tended garden that we had also created while our beautiful and extremely well-behaved children played together. We would have old and new friends over at the weekends and entertain them with amazing and delightful meals. We would live close to family who would remain healthy and available so they could look after our gorgeous children when we wanted to go away for a relaxing weekend. We would own one modest car, but have lots of time and money left for hobbies and play.

Reality was entirely different. I married a pastor. We didn't own a house, we were given one and then told by others what we could and could not do with it. Our furniture was given, second-hand and mismatched. We couldn't afford a decent car and we were given a wreck that should have been scrapped. Our garden was regularly dug up by our wild and difficult dog. Our children were always beautiful to us but they didn't play quietly. They were tiring and messy and hated what I cooked. They had inherited strong wills and loud voices. I had never thought they might inherit some of our worst traits, especially not mine. I had never thought it would take me six long winter months and lots of wet clothes hanging on radiators trying to get them dry and lots of tears (mine) to potty train them. I couldn't believe they took two hours to fall asleep.

I never thought that I would become obsessive about how many hours of continuous sleep I had and that I would count not only my hours of sleep but how many Mike had, and would hate it (and show it) if he had had more.

I never thought I would live in a area of London where crime was an everyday occurrence, where Mike and I were the only married people in our congregation, as there were only forty attending and most were single mothers or over 60. And in that place, I never thought I would feel called and compelled to take in an abandoned 13-year-old girl who warmed herself at night outside our church on the heater which I could see from my kitchen window.

I never thought I would live so far away from our parents and their support.

Perhaps I never thought at all.

But more than anything, I never thought that one day Mike would find me sobbing on the kitchen floor saying that I couldn't do it any more and that I had reached the end of my own strength and ability to cope.

Being bright, sweet and educated was not enough to get me through each day. All of my expectations and unrealistic dreams had been dashed onto the rocks of real life. Every single hope and dream had been stripped away.

My situation was not unique. Many of you reading this chapter will have thought that things would be different. You were led to believe that if you worked hard, looked pretty and said the right things, dreams would become a reality. If you followed all the formulas, took the right steps, life would work out. Maybe your parents said that you could and should live your dreams: 'You can do it!' Maybe teachers said you were really clever and that the world needed your skills. Maybe you were popular and had lots of friends. Whatever happened to being given the desires of your heart? Getting up off the floor that day, I learned I'd need to rely on God. I could not do it: I could not do this life. Yet His grace and strength were enough for each day and were so much more than my human strength and abilities. I didn't need to work harder, try harder with my life. I needed to develop and maintain a meaningful connection with Him.

I brought into my life disciplines that I knew would hold me when I became overwhelmed. I brought in rest and recreation. I brought in a time of prayer. I didn't sit for hours in silence. I prayed as I cleaned, I prayed as I pushed the buggy, I prayed as I cooked. I prayed when I felt inadequate for the tasks of mother and wife.

I took my hurts, my life, my hope, my all to the cross and I left them there. And at the cross, in the death and resurrection of Jesus, by the power of His Spirit, I received the grace I needed for each wonderful or impossible day.

Where did life unexpectedly interrupt your journey and bring you to your knees, be it in joy or pain? Before moving into the final section of the book, we invite you to pause for a while and invite Jesus into the situation you are in.

For some of us we'll pause simply to celebrate and worship, with thanksgiving and awe for His unexpected blessings that we know we didn't earn. We've been reminded that our God is faithful, gracious, compassionate, true.

For others we pause because we can't move any more. We can't find words to express all that is inside us and we're sobbing on our own personal kitchen floor, grieving the loss of the life we hoped for. He needs no words or declarations, because *He knows*. And He cares, carrying the weight of your storm, your grief and sorrow all the way to the cross for you (Isa. 53).

So for now we'll put our plans, suggestions and thoughts to the side. We'll meet you in another chapter at a later stage. More than anything or anyone, right now we need Him.

Take some time to be with Jesus, and invite Him into your life's unexpectedness. He'll meet you there.

12

Life watching

Being a girl is certainly easier than being a woman. Girls don't have to take responsibility for their destiny.
(Dr Lois Frankel)[1]

NOT AGAIN

I hated the sense of foreboding, the predictability of my impending failure. It was during the Christmas season I realised I needed to pay close attention to my life. I was gearing up to yet another year of pointless resolutions that I would fail to keep, disillusion that this New Year would be no different from any other. While nothing was terribly wrong, I was definitely stuck in a rut – in my relationships, in the career, in life in general. Even in my walk with the Lord. I had never expected that everything would be wonderful all the time, but too many things were simply not working, habitually, and that forced me to take notice. This year had to be different, but unless I looked at my life more closely I wouldn't be able to tell where things were going wrong (or, more often, going nowhere). I looked at the usual suspects: my prayer life, my Bible study, my church involvement, my relationships. But I'd done that before – I needed to go further. I was tired of going round in circles year after year. Not again.

It was a familiar parable that would bring me another step towards clarity. In Mark 4 Jesus told His listeners the parable of the sower. A farmer scattered seed which landed in different environments, yielding very different results. Jesus explained that the farmer planted the word. There was seed that fell on a hard path and was devoured by the birds, a symbol of the people who hear God's word but fail to hold on to it as Satan snatches it away. Some seed landed on shallow soil but failed to take root. These are the people who initially respond to God's word with enthusiasm but do not dig deep enough to withstand difficult times. They can't get beyond the high. Other seeds fell among weeds and thorns. These are the people who hear God's word, but their lives are so cluttered by worries, anxieties, worldly thinking and distracting desires that the clutter simply chokes the life out of them. Finally some seeds landed in good soil – those who hear what God is saying and respond, with exponential effects in their lives.

The parable read my life (and continues to do so!) and I was found wanting. I could connect with every type of seed, but it was the seeds that fell among weeds and thorns that seemed to resonate most this time.

So I started looking at some ordinary things – my health, how I ate and drank, my bank balance, my energy levels and how I spent my time. My job, my clothes. To say it was illuminating was an understatement. My life was chaotic, driven by poor time management, which in turn was driven by internal impulses to please and to prove something to others. Other areas were dictated to by immature ideas or bad habits, or ancient aches and wounds. Other areas I just avoided because denial was much more comfortable. My heart's desire for some order, and the call to personal transformation and maturity, was choked out by a lifestyle that was not immoral but was utterly unkempt. It was choking the life out of me, *His life* out of me. What good was my theology, my Bible studies, if God's words to me couldn't even impact my daily existence? Since when was my faith purely an intellectual belief system or just a salve for past hurts? Wasn't walking with Jesus supposed to define *my whole life*? It was beginning to look as though God was only able to impact my lifestyle choices on the big stuff we all talk about, like men, alcohol and tithing. I could no longer hear His voice in the ordinary stuff, like my time and the rest of my money, or my health or work. I couldn't sense His hand leading and shaping those areas either. Yet it wasn't that He was far away; this was no dark night of the soul or wilderness experience. But the cluttered thinking and feelings, the avoidance, the immaturity, the old habits, simply stood in the way of anything He would seek to bring into my life. Now He had my attention! I'd not seen my life this clearly and comprehensively before.

WATCH YOUR LIFE CLOSELY

One of the people the apostle Paul walked through life with was Timothy, a young man converted in his teens through Paul's ministry. Timothy eventually becomes one of Paul's trusted team – and more than that, he is like a son to Paul. The apostle is a discipling voice in Timothy's life, investing in him as Timothy grows into his roles within the New Testament church. Paul advises and instructs in many areas of ministry life, but also speaks directly to Timothy the man, the young adult, his character and values. He reminds him to train himself to be godly, illustrating the personal responsibility we have when it comes to investing in our relationship with God. One of the instructions he gives to Timothy as part of his training is to 'Watch your life and doctrine closely. Persevere in them, because if you do, you will save both yourself and your hearers' (1 Tim. 4:16).

The call to pay close attention to doctrine was to be expected, as Timothy ministers and leads in a permissive cultural context. Much of Paul's letter concerns the content of teaching in the Ephesian community that Timothy oversees. Paul speaks beyond first-century Ephesus; his words remind us today to keep allowing Scripture to define and refine our lives, rather than adapting it for personal comfort. Yet it's Paul's call to Timothy to *watch his life* that stays with me: the insistence that Timothy should *persevere in doing so*, and the impact it will have on Timothy's life *and* his wider community. Timothy needed to engage and take responsibility, and so do we. We cannot simply 'assume the position' again when it comes to everyday life, hoping, wishing, waiting for someone else to fix or live our lives on our behalf. Our lives need to be watched and worked at, because they are watched and are a testimony to the people around us.

We've explored scriptural truths that lie at the heart of our relationship with God and at the core of our identity. We've walked along the landscape of many of our significant relationships, both real and desired, and brought wounds and longings to light. But we also need to look at and to engage with life practically. Our spiritual life exists not just in our minds and hearts, but in our everyday lives. Here is where all that's happening on our insides is externalised, made real, and actually makes a difference. Any of us can talk a good game, and probably do, but in the end our walk speaks so much louder. And when I say walk I don't just mean the moments we walk into church or some Christian event. I mean the 24/7 days we live. When we watch our lives closely we find they're speaking all the time. We might already guess this to be true in our relationships, but there's more of life to watch and listen to. Our eating and drinking habits speak. The way we dress speaks. The language we use and the content of our conversations speak. How we spend our money, how we spend our time, speaks. The way we approach big decisions and our future speaks. So what is your life saying? Does it speak of a peaceful heart with a secure perspective, or someone defined by fear, anxiety or addictions? Does it point to a life put on hold or to a go-getter? Does it say that God is most important in your life, or does it say your possessions or popularity define and shape you? Is your life choking His life out of you?

Twenty-first-century living is often so fast and so full that it's easy to miss the signs that we need to pay attention to. Consequently we're unaware that our everyday choices – or lack of them – can point to something deeper beneath the surface of our existence.

It's time to make a spiritual discipline of taking the time to observe and engage with life's practicalities.

There are a number of reasons for doing this:

- God cares about the practical details of our lives. Walking with Him means walking with Him in the everyday ordinary stuff and inviting Him to be Lord of those areas. God wants to be involved in our money, our sleeping patterns, our career choice, because He wants and desires to be intimately involved with us.
- Sometimes the ways we engage with or avoid practical spheres of our lives are an indicator of an area that we need to allow the Lord to work on. In each area we explore we need to ask ourselves whether we engage or avoid, and to look at why.
- When our lives are too full or chaotic, it can choke His life out of our lives. We miss out when we miss Him.

Our lives are always saying something. So what is your life saying? And what would you like it to say?

When we disciple women, we always arrive at the topic of how we are engaging practically with our lives. This chapter draws on some of the ideas from the life review I began that Christmas season, a practice that I've continued in various forms for a number of years. It also draws on Sally's many life experiences and insights as a discipler. One of my favourite things about Sally is that her walk with Jesus is incredibly practical, her faith is *lived*. Our aim is to get you thinking and praying through a list of five key areas we often end up talking about with women we disciple. We also offer a few suggestions to get you started with some plans. When you've read the chapter and have an overview, it may well be worth block-ing out some time to go through each section in detail. It would be easy to read the following all in one sitting, and then to feel guilty about where you fall short but too overwhelmed to know where to start. If you are going to take an audit of your life, you need time to engage with the question, seek God and work things through. Take it as slowly as you need to. Perhaps you could block out a day for yourself to look at all five areas, or one evening a week for the next five weeks.

As you go through our list of areas in detail, keep the following questions in mind:

Q. When I look at this part of my life, what do I see? What's happening?

> **Do I avoid or fully engage with this area of my life? Why?**

> **What is God saying to me about this? Do I need to make some time to listen to Him, or is it already clear? Do I need to pray with some friends as I try to discern what God is saying about my life?**

> **What am I going to do about what I discover?**

ENGAGING PRACTICALLY? OUR BIG FIVE

1 Get a (healthy rhythm of) life!

'Hurry is not just a disordered schedule. Hurry is a disordered heart' (John Ortberg).[2]

Do you live a hurried life? Ever gone to sleep and woken up more tired than you were before you went to bed? Ever felt so beyond tired that you are worn out to the bone and feel perpetually on the edge? Is your body constantly run down because it never rests? Do you keep on getting ill with stress-related complaints? Have you adopted/indulged in some unhealthy habits to escape from the tiredness? Don't you find it strange that though the

Western world appears to have so many time-saving resources and devices – fast food, internet banking, instant entertainment, smart phones – we're still poverty-stricken when it comes to time?

Our lives are full, often too full. We have jobs, relationships and activities all vying for our attention, and often the tyranny of the urgent is the only winner. We work extra long hours, sometimes because we have to, sometimes because we need to, but sometimes because we don't know how to say no or stand up for ourselves. It's not just work either; we take on additional responsibilities in every area of life because we like to help others, or need to. As a result our lives become boundary-less, one day and all its *stuff* bleeding into the next. Furthermore, our hearts and minds are full. Something happened at work, at home, a difficult conversation, a challenging situation, but there's no time to process it, or no one has time to process it with you. TV, social media, things we normally enjoy, now just fill our minds with more thoughts, more things. There is less head and heart space.

It's difficult to make good decisions when we are tired. It's so much easier to eat the extra portion of junk food, to drink the extra glass or two of wine, to hang out with that guy we know is not a good idea. We might spend more in the shops because we can't be bothered to or haven't time to think about our budget. Our perspective is blunted when we are overtired, tempers fray more easily, negative thought patterns exist in our minds more freely, temptation tantalises more readily. The strength to stand under pressure or run away from bad choices seems to drain away.

The hardest thing, though, is that the pace of life we keep is rarely about time at all. We may need to develop some time management skills, but there are also reasons we overwork, over-commit, seek to overachieve in every part of our life. We might just be too focused on work at the expense of the rest of our lives because it's easier, we know we're competent there. We might be workaholics, literally addicted to working. We could be putting in extra hours trying to avoid pain, loneliness or difficulty at home. We might be perfectionists desperate to prove that we can be all things to all people. Perfectly. We might be driven by our past in other ways, determined to make a better life for ourselves, oblivious to the personal cost.

Is life choking His life out of you? Are His words of peace and grace to you tangled in the weeds and thorns of our culture and a mindset that tells you your value is found in what you do and accomplish?

His rhythm

'The true sign of godliness – imitating God – is to pattern our lives after him. And for God, rest is vitally important'.[3]

God made us for a different way of living. Yes, we are *ezer*s designed and called for relationship and purpose in this world, called to productive living. Yet when we look back at humanity's first experience on earth, we learn that their first experience was rest. They were created on the sixth day and their first day was with God and one another. From the place of being with God and being in community flowed the momentum to do the work of representing God in the world. Does the activity in your life flow from your connection with God, and your primary relationships? Do they define how much you do? Or does busyness come first, cramming in God and people when and where you can? (Equally, do you allow the momentum of your relationship with God, and your faith community to push you outwards, into representing Him in the world where He's placed you? More on that in the following chapter.)

God cares so much about our rest that in Exodus 20 it's number four in the Ten Commandments. God commands everybody to take a day off in the week. Yet do we take it as seriously as we do other commandments further down on the list – murder, adultery, stealing? Do we take a day a week to rest and recharge?

Jesus illustrated these values in His own life. He was constantly in demand: entire villages and towns would seek Him out, bringing their sick and hurting, longing for leadership and hope in the vacuum of their lives. Can you imagine the pressure to cave in to what was expected, even out of compassion for the people? Yet Jesus knew who He was and what He was there for. He would not be swayed from His mission, His focus would not be blurred. There was a rhythm to the way He lived that flowed from His walk with the Father, not the demands of the world around Him. So He would pull away to be alone with His Father. He would gather His disciples and spend time and invest in them even if a village had arrived to see Him. He knew His priorities. And then He ministered, taught, healed, delivered, saved a broken world. His life demonstrated not a brittle rigid system, but a rhythm worth imitating.

It might seem odd that this is the first of our Big Five things.

But we all know that we make healthier decisions about every area of life when we are fully rested. With a peaceful mind, an unhurried heart and a refreshed body we are far more equipped to respond to the challenges and opportunities of twenty-first-century living. But that won't happen to us automatically. We need to make room in our lives to make that happen. And we'll probably need to get a little ruthless about it too.

I could always justify being busy. There was always a reason why my life needed to be as overcommitted as it was. So it was instrumental to have Sally alongside me at this point to be both objective and ruthless when needed. I was too emotionally involved to discern anything at all.

We discussed my key priorities. What were the most important areas in my life? Who was most important? What did rest look like for me? How did I recharge?

We looked at my week and blocked a day off. We looked at my month to pre-empt pressure points. Did I need a retreat day? A fun day? What would recharging look like?

We looked at the year and blocked out holidays, spread out across the year. And she held me accountable for following through on the decisions I'd made.

It felt great and awful at the same time. Great because there was space to breathe, to heal, to rest. Awful because I worried about letting people down, letting God down, being missed, not being missed (!). Still, it was absolutely essential to deal with the attitudes that kept bringing me to the brink of burn-out and choked God's life out of me.

Over the years, as the seasons of life change, I've learned to return and keep returning to the principles I learned then. My life looks different and in some ways is more complex now. How do you apply these principles when you are married or have kids? The world's pace does not seem to change – in fact it seems more driven than ever! It's so easy for me to be drawn into over-activity; there is always something to do and it's the relentless doing that makes me lose my way. Though it is a battle sometimes, I can't afford to let my life lack rest and refreshment. I can't afford to miss out on His voice and peace. I can't afford to neglect the relationships He has given me. When I work on living God's rhythm for my life, there is a time for everything that matters in that season, and there is a freedom to let go of the things that just won't fit. There is rest and wholeness and my mind is clearer.

Q. Do you avoid taking time off? Why?
Do you need to learn to rest and recharge?

A few ideas to get you started:

- Write out a copy of your current weekly timetable. If you don't have one, record what each day looks like over a seven-day period. How are you currently spending your time? Where is it going well? Where is it going badly?

- Show your timetable to a close friend or mentor – and invite them to comment on what they see.
- Look again at your timetable. How can you best prepare for the busy/stressful parts of your week? Do you need to commit to a weekly day off? Look also at where you can acknowledge the call to rest in your timetable. Think about how you enjoy resting and recharging. You could also expand this to look at the month, even the year, so that you can see any potential challenges in advance (though we can't plan everything: life still offers the unexpected) and blocking out holiday time and fun getaways well in advance.
- Take a look at your priorities. We believe that your relationship with God comes first, then your key relationships, then your job and other activities beyond that. It's not that you necessarily carve up your time in percentages, but if our relationships are important, for example, then that should be reflected somehow in how we spend our time.
- Recognise that we don't need to and can't 'have it all', especially not all at once. If you are going to incorporate times of rest and relaxation into your life then you will need to take other things out of your life. Again, it's vital to have someone to process this area with.
- Take note of the emotions that rise to the surface when you step back from over-commitment. Is it guilt, fear, failure, relief? What do you think God wants to say to you?
- If you have young children, you often need the support of a wider community to help you get the space and rest you need. Who likes you and your family? Who can you trust?

Top tip: Learn how to say no. As an intermediate step you could say, 'I'll think about it' or 'I'll get back to you', but you may have to spend the next few weeks avoiding that person. 'No' is easier in the end.

Q. What is God saying to you? What do you need to do about it?

2 Money

'For the love of money is a root of all kinds of evil' (1 Tim. 6:10). There are more than two thousand verses in the Bible about money, wealth and possessions, many more than most subjects we pay much more attention to, like prayer or Bible study. Money can bring freedom but it can also bring heartache and headaches, regardless of how much you have. It can create opportunities for homes and cars and mission trips, or reveal our limitations. How we engage with money is a spiritual thing. Money is powerful, and has such a powerful effect on our lives that it is easy to make money our god, our security, our ultimate desire and our highest priority. We can slip into thinking money is the answer to life's problems. Jesus gives His disciples a reality check: 'No one can serve two masters. Either you will hate the one and love the other, or you will be devoted to the one and despise the other. You cannot serve both God and Money' (Matt. 6:24).

How do we engage practically with our finances? No one has been immune to the economic challenges of recent years. According to research by Credit Action,

- In the UK, 197 mortgage possession claims will be issued and 154 mortgage possession orders will be made today.
- In the UK, 383 landlord possession claims will be issued and 258 landlord possession orders will be made today.

Still, they also note:

- 25.2m plastic card purchase transactions will be made in the UK today, with a total value of £1.278bn.

In conjunction with uSwitch they also note that students have an average debt of £21,198 when they finish university, which takes eleven years on average to clear. This in turn leads to a delay in big decisions like marriage and having children.

When I'm talking with other women, we are constantly processing the power money has over our lives. One longs to be a stay-at-home mum, but the house they bought means she has to work full-time. Should they move to a new home in a cheaper part of the country or was she just living in a fantasy, thinking she could have all she wanted? Another wonders whether it is wise to invest so much in today's lifestyle and the things you desire without paying attention to the future. Is it fair to expect that one day your husband will provide for you, thinking that 'getting married' is a good feasible financial plan? Or is your financial plan reliant on receiving an inheritance?

How do you handle money? Do you avoid it or engage with it? Are you so used to your student debts in the background that you don't face what to do about them? Is that OK? Does your desire for a certain lifestyle and possessions shape your use of credit cards? Does God have a say in how you spend your money? Do you own money or does it own you, either by your desires or by your avoidance?

How to engage:

Engage with our emotions on money

Again, we need to observe our behaviour. How does money make you feel? Does spending give you a bit of a rush? Spending is like a nice girl's drug. Do you feel comforted, in control of your future? Is the plastic card the solution to a tough day at the office or a sad day at home? Does it give you the power to buy the identity you want through clothes, shoes and possessions? And have you connected with God on these feelings?

Engage with God on money

Engaging with God is not just about tithing and offerings, though we'll reflect upon that. We have surrendered our entire lives to God, which includes all of our money, not merely a percentage. Does God own your purse? This is not just about depositing the right amount into the offering plate. We can do that legalistically and still not have engaged with God on money. This is about how we trust Him above all else and how we remain permanently open to God on how we handle money.

> *Sally: Through the years we've adopted the following pattern to help us with our money:*
>
> *Ask – We pray about our money, needs and resources.*
>
> *Give – We give our tithes and our offerings.*
>
> *Save – We saved for big things and small things, for weddings and holidays, for furniture. Saving means you live within your means and not just by your desires. Saving means you build towards your future too, or can give away lump sums of money to anyone God calls you to. Save something, anything! You never know what you might need it for in the days to come.*
>
> *Share – A great way not to be owned by money and possessions is to share things! We shared homes, cars, clothes, meals.*
>
> *Spend – Well, you know what that means! Splash out on others from time to time. Be generous, and enjoy God's provision for you!*

And tithes and offerings? I love the fact that there is this one place where God invites us to test Him, and it concerns money. In the book of Malachi, God speaks through the prophet, confronting His people for robbing Him through not giving tithes (10 per cent of their income) and offerings. He offers this challenge:

> 'Bring the whole tithe into the storehouse, that there may be food in my house. Test me in this,' says the Lord Almighty, 'and see if I will not

throw open the floodgates of heaven and pour out so much blessing that there will not be room enough to store it. I will prevent pests from devouring your crops, and the vines in your fields will not drop their fruit before it is ripe,' says the LORD Almighty. 'Then all the nations will call you blessed, for yours will be a delightful land,' says the LORD Almighty. (Mal. 3:10–12)

Have you put God to the test by learning how to tithe, and looked to see His provision and resources, financial and otherwise? It's an experiment that I'd like to encourage you to try to help you discover who is the better provider. Try giving God 10 per cent of your income, setting up a standing order from your account.

There we find that He is still our stronger covenant partner and as such our provider. He is the source of all we need. And He offers to protect our resources, and provide in such a way that our blessing is a witness to others. We don't like to talk about money, even when God blesses us, just in case it sounds as if we're boasting. Yet when God provides for us we don't give witness to ourselves: we are testifying that our God provides for our needs because He is a kind and loving and powerful Father. That is worth sharing, because it tells others not about what we've got, but about *who* He is and how He moves in people's lives today.

Engage with the experts on money

Whether you feel you're good with money or weak with money, there are many good resources out there that can help you engage. Your resource might come in the form of a friend who is good with money and who knows how to do a budget. If you're married it might be that you and your spouse have different approaches to money, and different skills. Within your general approach to money, work to your strengths. There are some great books on money management. Credit Action have some fantastic resources for a wider range of financial issues.

Rather than avoid it, get financial advice, and don't wait until you're married to get it. Talk through investments, pensions, property. And don't wait until you are married to make decisions about buying a car or a house. It's not about being old or selling out from spontaneity. It's about taking responsibility as a woman. It's not that you have to do all these things, but you need to be equipped now to help you to make informed choices and decisions about your future. You might learn that you need them when it's way too late.

Q. What is God saying to you? What do you need to do about it?

3 Healthy body

'Do you not know that your bodies are temples of the Holy Spirit?' writes Paul, concluding, 'Therefore honour God with your bodies' (1 Cor. 6:19–20). When did you last pay attention to your health? Are you sleeping well? Are you drinking too much alcohol? Take a look at your diet. Are you eating well, eating healthy balanced meals, with healthy portion sizes? Have you been to the dentist recently? Do you smoke? How well are you looking after your body?

Perhaps these incessant questions sound like the unwelcome voice of a nagging mother! When we were girls it was their job to look after our bodies, to arrange our dental and optician's appointments, to make sure we were eating well. Now that we are women, we need to take responsibility for things like our health and diet. It's our job to look after ourselves and to get enough sleep; it's our job to look at what we eat and drink and look after our bodies. We don't want to obsess about our weight – after all, age and changes like babies can *fundamentally* change our bodies. Still, if you've noted significant weight loss or gain in recent times, it's worth thinking about. Get a notebook to chart what you eat and how you feel for a week or two and see what it tells you. Some of us develop allergies that fundamentally affect our bodies, our menstrual cycle, our energy levels. I gave up wheat and dairy for Lent and was staggered at how alive I felt. It was disorienting, but began a process of eliminating gluten from my food and feeling much clearer and much more energised as a result. Some of us have come out of painful histories with eating disorders, obesity, cutting. Be honest about how it affects you today and seek out support if you need it.

Look after yourself. Check with your doctor about how to do regular breast examinations, when to have mammograms. Have a cervical smear. Find a form of exercise that you love and commit to it. This is your body and you only have one to last you for the rest of your life. Celebrate it and look after it!

Q. What is God saying to you? What do you need to do about it?

4 Your personal presentation: think high heels and holiness

One of my favourite TV shows of all time is *What Not to Wear* (it's no longer shown in the UK, but the US version is still going strong). The weekly scenario is as follows: an unsuspecting style-challenged woman is given the opportunity to revolutionise her wardrobe at the hands of fashion stylists who manage to be incredibly blunt and affirming at the same time. It's often a painful and difficult journey for the woman involved, but by the end of the experience the individual looks radiant, with new clothes and a whole new look. Interestingly, in the interviews that follow, these women often talk about an inner transformation that has taken place as well. The young woman who is no longer a student now embraces her life as a woman at work who is worth taking seriously. The young mum comes to terms with her post-baby weight and finds a new look for who she is today. The everywoman with no particular crisis, who embraces her womanhood and expresses it articulately in how she looks, presents herself in a new way, and her community, her family and her colleagues take notice.

Perhaps it seems superficial and worldly, but how we present ourselves matters and affects our lives. We want people to take us seriously because we have incredible insights, passion and wisdom. We want people to see our competence and character above anything else. It's a valid desire, but it's naive to think that how we present ourselves does not affect how we are perceived. Studies suggest that the vast majority of communication is found not in our actual words but in non-verbal cues. Some of that is achieved in our tone of voice, our smile, our posture, the way we give other people attention and express interest in them. Some of it, like it or not, is communicated in our appearance, our look, our hair-style, our clothing. Since we communicate so much in the way we present ourselves, it's worth periodically reviewing what we are actually saying! Sometimes we are not aware of the messages we present to others.

We have to be honest with ourselves. Why do we dress the way we do? What is your look, the way you communicate, your ward-robe, saying? Is it saying, 'Don't notice me because I'm inadequate'? Does it scream, 'Notice me and notice my sexuality', because that's how you have learned to get what you want? Does it communicate an era of your life when you were younger and happier, one that you are unwilling to let go of, or does it reflect and celebrate the woman God has made you and the life that you live with Him today? For many years my clothes were about hiding, hiding my perceived shape, hiding from people. At other times my clothes said I was grieving. In a particular stage it was about a defiant sexu-ality and giving people a bit too much information! But what I have noticed is that how I dress is rarely about nothing: it's been an illustration of my sense of worth and value. I've needed to invite the Lord into the heart issues and mindsets which lie behind my wardrobe. If you had a *What Not to Wear* type transformation, what would it reveal? One reason that I love the show so much is that it's a picture of redemption in a woman's life, an echo of the type of healing Jesus offers us every day. So why not let Him bring that to you too? Now we all have different styles and preferences, and that is a wonderful creative thing. Our jobs determine how we look too. We don't need to be Christian clones and call it holiness. But I would encourage us to be conscious dressers, aware of the messages we are communicating.

So, if you want to work on your wardrobe a little, where do you start?

We'll start with a caveat! The challenge we face as we do this is that, as we flick through magazines and websites as a resource, we buy into the messages of our culture on body shape and consumerism. On a positive note, these resources draw from some incredibly creative artistic minds that have an eye for colour and beauty and appreciate the female form. Yet we hold that alongside the fact that these resources also cultivate images of life and beauty for our aspiration and entertainment (and frankly, sales), *not reality*. We know that airbrushing is a common feature of the pictures we see, so not even the models really look like the pictures they are in! We understand that wearing that particular perfume will not mean that a bronzed Adonis will drape himself over our bodies in order to sniff us. We know that this moisturiser will not make our legs cellulite-free and that dress will not make our arms look defined and toned. So, with a dose of humour and lots of common sense and wisdom, here are

Some sartorial suggestions

- Dress for the shape and size that you are, not the one you aspire to. That might mean it's time to embrace your body shape. Use magazines and websites to get some good suggestions on what might suit you.

- Rather than keeping on buying things that you will never wear, work out what your essential items are. Sally's include a crisp white shirt, a great pair of jeans and a pretty summer dress for the wedding season. Jo's are a good pair of black trousers, a V-neck sweater and a good pair of shoes. What are your basic essentials?
- If you're not sure what to wear at work, look around your office. Executive coach Lois Frankel says, 'Look around at the successful women in senior positions in your organisation. *That's* how you should dress.'[4] She recommends that you dress for the job you want, not the job you have.[5]
- Do your research. What colours look good on you? Maybe you could have your colour palette done, or simply ask a friend who has an eye for colour. Don't feel afraid to ask for fashion advice from a trusted friend, a mentor, people in the store where you're shopping. I have been saved by many a retail assistant who simply knew better than I did. Who said we were supposed to know all about this, anyway?
- Rule of thumb: if your teenage daughter/sister would wear it, you shouldn't. If members of your youth group are wearing it, you really shouldn't. I remember the day I realised I and one of the youth group were wearing the same thing – it just didn't feel right or good. It wasn't about who wore it better, it was the revelation that either she was dressing pretty adult or I was dressing like a tweenager. (I call this the 'mutton dressed as lamb' situation, one of my deepest sartorial fears.) Some of us pull this off and some of us have a new opportunity for shopping. Mine was definitely the latter. Sally, who is great at this stuff and came up with most of these suggestions, recommends that we develop a style but review it every twenty-four months. What is a great style when you are 21 is not good when you are a 28-year-old mother of two toddlers.
- Invest in good underwear. If you are, ahem, well endowed, a

good bra is a gift that keeps on giving and well worth the expense. Get a bra fitting to find out your actual size, and invest well. You'll never short-change *the girls* again.

- Shop within your means. We don't have to buy into consumerist thinking on clothing. Set a budget for your clothes and stick to it; save up for investment pieces that are worth paying more for, and check out high-quality second-hand stores. Make the most of the sales; share things with friends.

- Clear out of your wardrobe the things you've not worn for a year and you know you won't wear again. If those clothes are no longer your size, don't live in denial any more. Take a trip to the local charity shop and let them go.

- A little make-up can add a lot to your look, so learn how to use it well. Make the most of the make-up floor at a department store and get as much advice (and free samples!) as you can.

- Get a good hairdresser who knows what they are doing. Get recommendations from people who have great hair. And when you are with your hairdresser, be assertive about what you want. After all, you have to pay for it and live with it! You don't have to become a creative experiment.

Are you willing to engage with how you present yourself to the world around you?

Q. What is God saying to you? What do you need to do about it?

5 Engage with your future

Finally, we want to encourage you, urge you, to face and engage with your future. Your life is not waiting for you to be discovered. It's not waiting for you to wake up. Don't drift along through this life expecting everything you want to just happen for you. Life is not waiting until you find your perfect job/get married/have kids/lose a stone. It's happening now. There will be twists and turns and disappointments; not all your dreams will come true. It's highly likely that your fantasies won't ever come true. And even when some of your desires do work out, this often happens in ways you don't expect. So please don't let it pass you by: embrace this gift called life that God has given you!

Whatever you anticipate for your future, in relationships, work, church, will require that you engage with it at some level today. With this in mind, we'll ask you some questions that have already appeared in one form or another in this book.

Are there things you are not doing because you are still waiting for life to happen? Not buying a house or car, not investing in your gifts or career or pursuing God's call on your life? Waiting until you feel ready, feel secure, are in a preferred life stage . . .?

It's time to think practically about your future. It might be overwhelming, but the good news is you don't have to do this alone. You have your covenant partner. Some of us already know it's time to stop procrastinating or fantasising about the life we want, even feel called to, and to start engaging in some way. But how do you engage with your future?

It sounds obvious, but prayer is the place to start. Since God knows the plans He has for us (Jer. 29:11), it makes sense that we take note of any direction He might offer. As you pray, listen for verses of Scripture that come to mind. Pray for opportunities to open up for you. Sometimes God's guidance is evident in the desires in our hearts and the thoughts in our minds. Still, we want to do more than dream and imagine; some of us have got stuck in this stage and it's time for action.

Invite the wisdom of trusted friends and family who know you well enough to speak into your situation. These are people who see your gifts and skills and qualities. They also know your weaknesses. What potential do they see in you, that you are currently not engaging with? Perhaps they also have insights into the areas of your life which seem to be on hold. Maybe they would speak to you about the attitudes that hold you back: it won't always make comfortable listening but it could help bring some much-needed clarity on where you are now. The Father Himself might be speaking through those conversations.

You pray about it, and then you start to make some plans. Practical, specific plans. Rather than waiting until you are 100 per cent sure, you start moving and make a journey of discovery. Your plans will involve some kind of action.

Some of us work best by thinking of where we want to be in five years' time and working backwards. So if there is a particular level you want to reach in your career five years from now, you consider what that means for the life you live today. It could mean that you start saving today, because you are going to need to study to get more qualifications. You might talk to HR and see what training courses are available within the context of work. You might decide it's time to pursue a mentor or coach to help you develop the skills you need that will build towards your future.

You might decide that in five years you want to own your own house. Well, perhaps that means that today you need to come up with some plans for getting rid of your debt, and you might need to earn some extra income.

For some of us, thinking five years ahead seems impossibly restrictive because it's too open-ended. So much can happen in that time that the future doesn't help us make sense of the present until we break it down into more manageable specific steps. So break it down: maybe five years from now you would like to be in full-time missionary work. That means that next summer you might spend a few weeks on a short-term mission. It might mean that in the next month you get in touch with some mission organisations. In the next week you could talk to a friend who's been on mission. Or that even today you start praying and browsing some sites of missionary organisations. They are small tangible steps, and you might add to them or adapt them along the way as life sees fit – but life is on the move.

Q. What is God saying to you? What do you need to do about it?

Don't spend your life going in circles, imagining what life could be but doing nothing to get there. Watch your life closely. Make a spiritual discipline of taking the time to observe and engage with life's practicalities. Look at your Big Five (or any other areas that come to mind) and choose to engage with the life God has given you and with faith that is lived.

> So here's what I want you to do, God helping you: Take your every-day, ordinary life – your sleeping, eating, going-to-work, and walking-around life – and place it before God as an offering. Embracing what God does for you is the best thing you can do for him. Don't become so well-adjusted to your culture that you fit into it without even thinking. Instead, fix your attention on God. You'll be changed from the inside out. Readily recognize what he wants from you, and quickly respond to it. Unlike the culture around you, always dragging you down to its level of immaturity, God brings the best out of you, develops well-formed maturity in you.
> (Rom. 12:1–2, *The Message*)

13
On our watch

God is shaking his daughters awake and summoning us to engage. His vision for us is affirming and raises the bar for all of us. We cannot settle for less. We have work to do.
(Carolyn Custis James)[1]

I wonder what the news was on the Web, the paper, the TV, the radio, that you woke up to today.

Did it fill you with hope, or bring you despair? Were you angry or are you immune to whatever you hear?

Today, somewhere in your past when you read this, I woke up to news that there are riots in my home city of London. Ancient feuds have been rekindled, memories of injustice and questions as to whether the injustice ever left. Violence erupted on the streets, looting emptied stores around the city. Friends are tweeting that they are staying home tonight. In my current home, California, I woke up to yet another newsflash about US debts and the fragility of the global economy. Some are predicting another recession. Friends are Facebooking, wondering if they are out of the last recession yet and unleashing their opinions about political parties and their leaders, and tensions are rising. People who had little to begin with are losing everything. The smell of fear for the future is no longer faint; it's a stench. Other voices use social media to remind us of the people of Somalia, facing famine and devastation. And none of the stories are new. When you read this, those headlines will be old news and the world will have indeed moved on. There will be other priorities, other headlines, which themselves will only have their fleeting moment of fame, consideration or notoriety. Maybe that's what makes it so easy to click and watch the news disappear. Only this time there's a sentence running through my head which is particularly stubborn, refusing to be switched off.

This is happening on your watch.

These words call out like a lone prophetic voice, adopting a different tone each time. Sometimes it's a whisper, a reminder. Sometimes it's a bold cry. Most often it's incredulous, a question asking, then audaciously demanding, a response.

This is happening on your watch?

I hear it when I think of a multibillion-pound human trafficking industry. I hear it when I think that twenty-seven million are enslaved worldwide, many of them children, and that UNICEF notes that there are nearly two million children in the commercial sex trade. I think of it when I read that in the developing world 850 million people go to bed hungry every night, or that 20 per cent of the world has no access to clean water, that between 1.6 and 2.5 million children die of diarrhoea every year. Diarrhoea.[2] The question gets even louder when I remember that ten million children under 5 die each year from *largely preventable diseases*. I hear of it when I think of the Western world, seemingly so rich, yet poor and broken in many other ways. I think of it as I reflect on these recent years living in the USA, contrasting the greed and opulence of Wall Street with the broken wounded families clinging on to a life that they cannot afford: the stress of lost savings and investment, the empty homes, the closed businesses, the rising unemployment and with it shock and hopelessness and deep fear-filled grief.

This, all this, is happening *on your watch?*

It's jarring. On a Sunday for an hour or so I experience life-changing worship, incredible teaching, powerful ministry. I see brothers and sisters healed and set free. I hear testimonies of miracles, seriously serious miracles, that only God can give explanation to. I wonder about the chasm between the two worlds, and how to bridge the gap.

There was one other thing I read in the news today. Women are leaving the Church in America much faster than men. I know that Europe is miles ahead on those statistics of decline. In fact, in a recent visit to the UK a friend told me the statistics are true for England too. Women have had enough and are leaving the Church in droves for a range of reasons. So much for spirituality being a feminine girly thing. The women of the Western world did not get the memo to stick around.

This is happening. On your watch.

We've been walking for a while. You're not a stranger any more, you're a sister. We've taken in highs and lows together on the journey. There have been moments when it's been right to pause and rest, others when it's been right, though rather uncomfortable, to press on and dig deeper. But as our journey ends, there's one last thing that we're desperate for you to understand.

We may use our time differently, living very different lives, yet *we share the same watch.*

You see, every generation of Christians has a choice about how they will respond to the issues of their day, on their watch. We have been given life in all its fullness, we have encountered salvation, *we know God!* It must affect how we spend our days on this earth – how can it not? We know there is more to life than beauty and celebrity and physical attractiveness. We know there is more to humanity than the cars people drive, the homes they live in and the holidays they take. Each person on earth has been made in the image of God – and without His hand upon their life, the restlessness of life without Him remains in people's hearts, homes, communities and nations. How do we represent God in this world? Of course, we have different gifts and different opportunities, but Jesus' last words to His disciples then, and to His disciples now, were a commission to a shared calling.

Then Jesus came to them and said, 'All authority in heaven and on earth has been given to me. Therefore go and make disciples of all nations, baptising them in the name of the Father and of the Son and of the Holy Spirit, and teaching them to obey everything I have commanded you. And surely I am with you always, to the very end of the age.'

(Matt. 28:18–20)

We've often interpreted 'therefore go' as a special phrase for special missionaries. Yet the verse can also be translated 'As you are going . . .' We're reminded that God entrusted the incredible task of changing the world in His name, for His glory, to ordinary disciples then and ordinary disciples now. *We are all missionaries, sent ones.* You may not know exactly what God wants you to do, where God wants you to go. In the meantime though, as you are going . . . there are two things the Lord has definitely called you to: discipleship and mission.

MAKE DISCIPLES, WHO MAKE DISCIPLES, WHO MAKE DISCIPLES . . .

We began this book acknowledging the weariness of so many women who long to go for God, but have had no one who would walk on their journey. They don't know all the answers and don't expect anyone else to, just perhaps someone who is a few steps ahead. Someone they can see has resolved certain things in their life, someone whose life illustrates the *how* of following Jesus. A life perhaps worth imitating. Why couldn't that person be you? You are called to make disciples . . . who can you invest in, who can you pour your life into? You could ask how they are doing spiritually. Perhaps you could help them see the love of a Father and a covenant-making Saviour, share how you've cultivated your relationship with God. You could ask how they are doing relationally, processing friendship, love and commitment. You could ask, for all the talking and processing, how they will practically engage with their God-given life. Perhaps you can help them monitor their rhythm of life or share some budget tips. And you can help them see how the Great Commission applies to them too . . .

Sometimes the thought of it is hard for us. We've wanted that for years, and yes, we deserved it, but many of us were left learning things the hard way. But we all have an opportunity to be part of the solution now, to play our part in mobilising an army of passionate, God-filled believers who will learn to stand for Him, serve for Him and share the gospel for Him. We need disciples who are strong enough for the tough times that come with life, who through the tears will not walk away from Jesus, but stand and offer a sacrifice of praise. We need disciples who can wrestle with difficult questions in life and who, even when there is no neat and tidy answer, will walk with God, even if it's at a slower pace, and will not be polluted by cynicism. We need disciples with the capacity and character to make more disciple-making disciples who live by God's Word and operate in the power of the Spirit. We need you. We need you to live like a disciple, and to be a disciple-maker.

Who has God called you to disciple? What are you going to do about it?

DISCIPLESHIP LEADING TO MISSION

God's mission is that people come to know Him. Jesus walked the earth speaking the words of the good news of the kingdom of God, but also demonstrating the values of the kingdom. He confronted society's prejudices and demonstrated how God valued people. He walked in the power of the kingdom, healing the sick, delivering the oppressed, raising the dead. And He equipped His young followers to do exactly the same. The New Testament illustrates that when Jesus discipled people, it didn't result purely in more knowledge, it birthed a missional movement that changed the course of human history. When the young early church made disciples it grew from this tiny, insignificant, often maligned group on the margins to the religion of the Roman Empire within 300 years. Its members understood that they were a sent people, that discipleship within its very definition had a missionary calling. And as they were going, they served and they shared and they shared and they served.

Too many things are happening on our watch. We need disciples who will go to the inner cities, our forgotten neighbourhoods. We need disciples who will go to the rich and comfortable, who will walk along corridors of power and serve the true King – as Daniel and Joseph and Esther did in Scripture – whose careers will also be a missional calling whether they are in marketing or the media or are stay-at-home mums. We need disciples for whom the nations will be their home. We need women who will dare to rise up and be influential in their world . . . Will you be one of them?

INFLUENTIAL WOMEN

It's interesting to note that while we wrestle with what Christian women should, can and are allowed to do, the world around us has noted that women are incredibly influential and play a significant role in society. They've also noted that when women are not given equal opportunity in their society – be it in education, security, human rights – the entire community is affected. In 2010 the United Nations set up UN Women, a body for gender equality and women's empowerment, seeking to accelerate their goals and objectives for women in society. In *Half the Sky*, authors Nicholas D. Kristof and Sheryl WuDunn contend that educating girls plays a major role across the world in lowering birth rate, improving children's health and transforming society.[3] One way or another, they have seen the potential that lies within an *ezer*, made in the image of God.

Peter Greer from HOPE International (a global faith-based micro-financing organisation) notes that of their 300,000 entrepreneurs 80 per cent are women, pointing out that when a woman is helped to grow a business, much more of her income will go back into benefiting the community.

What could we be and do if we embraced our God-given design to make a difference for the glory of His name? Here is one woman's story that Peter shared with us:

As one of hundreds of thousands of orphans left in the wake of the 1994 Rwandan genocide, Chantal Nyiraneza knows the necessity of relying on God's care – and the joy of extending that care to others. Like so many Rwandans, Chantal found herself grieving the loss of her parents even as she faced the unexpected responsibility of caring for her two younger brothers and a cousin.

Rather than resenting her newfound responsibilities, Chantal saw them as opportunities to extend God's love. In the sixteen years since the genocide, she has continued to share this love, and the number of people she supports has only grown. Several years ago, she married another genocide survivor, whose two younger siblings joined the family. Together the couple adopted yet another orphan and had three biological children.

In order to help support their large family, Chantal started selling milk, sodas, and African tea to bicycle taxi riders and other passersby. A natural entrepreneur, Chantal soon saw that her limited menu was not attracting new customers. Undaunted, Chantal took out a HOPE loan of $35. With this money, she slowly began to introduce various food items to the menu, including roasted goat meat, fish, and chicken.

Just as Chantal predicted, business has increased exponentially with this expanded menu. Currently on her eighteenth loan, Chantal now roasts two goats a day to keep up with the demand of her 200 customers, and her restaurant makes more money each day than she took out in her original loan. Chantal's profits help provide food, clothes, and school fees for her nine children, and she has also built a new home that is large enough to comfortably house the entire family.

As Chantal's situation has improved, she has in turn been directly responsible for improving the lives of her community members. Over the years, her restaurant has employed twenty-eight people, and rather than viewing them as competition, she has encouraged each of them to use their experience at her restaurant to start their own business.

With her encouragement and help, twenty of them have done so, forming a community bank to take out HOPE loans themselves. Chantal glorifies God for her own success and the help she has been able to give these former employees. 'There is no way I could have changed my history without God's help. God has done this that you see today.' With God's help, Chantal dreams of expanding her business to other underserved areas, spreading the impact of her business to many more individuals and helping to rebuild her country one person at a time.[4]

Inspiring, isn't she? Chantal deployed her God-given gifts to serve her community. Lives were transformed and Chantal pointed to God in it all. It's important to look up and see a global picture.

But let's get back to your story, your journey, your influence. As a disciple you follow in the footsteps of One who continually overturned society's injustice. He loved the outcast, the broken, the nobodies. Will you follow Him there? Where will you use your gifts and talents, your willing heart, your time and energy to serve the King? Where will you make a difference? Will you invest your money into micro-financing, get involved in your church, go on a mission trip? And again, we don't have to do this alone. Jesus sent His disciples out in teams, and for the vast majority of the New Testament we see little groups responding to God's call.

How will we respond to what is happening on our watch? How will we engage practically?

Start praying, start talking with your friends and start exploring what is out there. And do something.

IT'S NECESSARY TO USE WORDS. SPEAK UP!

We also have a message to share, a Person to share, with the people around us.

Sally: I've been passionate about mission since my youth group days when we were given opportunities to share our faith in our community. I've been seeking opportunities to share my faith ever since. I started in Manchester, feeding the homeless and acting in evangelistic plays. In my twenties when I had small children I ran groups for parents and toddlers, I managed a nearly new clothes shop on the high street that brought in hundreds of people from our inner-city parish, and I helped set up a project that brought health visitors and nurses into the community by teaching parenting and basic care skills in our café. All of these things gave me and others on our teams an amazing opportunity to talk about our faith and our life stories to people who would never go inside a church or church building.

Later, in my time in Sheffield, I worked as a learning mentor and teaching assistant in one of the worst comprehensives in the city. When I started I was the only Christian on the staff team of seventy-five people. By the time I left I had managed to get another three Christians working in the school and our church had developed extremely effective children and youth outreach in the area. Ten years later, the church still has a strong presence in that community.

Now I live in the USA with completely different missional opportunities and challenges. I meet for a regular prayer time with several young, single women who have difficult and challenging lives and who wonder if God can change those lives. We meet in the local Starbucks where they work. I pray for breakthrough in their lives and remind them of a loving heavenly Father who cares for them. Whatever season or stage of life we're in, there is still a call to be missional in some way. Are you only spending time with Christians? Are you being intentional about the times you are spending with your non-Christian friends?

What is happening *as you are going*? For me right now, it's making friends with parents at the school gates, praying for them, looking to see who is currently receptive to the gospel. It's building relationships with our neighbours. It's talking through life with my hairdresser. It's being open to the fleeting moments that happen when you meet someone in the park or on a bus or train or plane. Mission can be a major trip to a foreign land or it can be working with drug addicts. It can also be meeting other co-workers for a drink after work and telling them what you're thankful to God for. The point is that we tell people about Jesus. We tell them because He has changed our lives and He will change theirs. We tell them because He is more than relevant to them, He is their Saviour. He is good news! We tell them because this is our watch. And it is our call.

WHERE DO WE START?

When Jesus sent His disciples out on mission in Luke 9 and 10 (see also Matthew 10) He advised them not to expend their energies on those who were not interested in them, but to look for the person of peace (Luke 10:6). The person of peace is someone who is open to you, someone who welcomes you and serves you, someone who is interested in you and who you are. Jesus calls the disciples to stay with those relationships, invest in them, minister to them, praying for healing and communicating the good news of the kingdom.

Who are the people of peace in your life? Are they friends, family members, work colleagues, people who don't know the Lord but who you have a great relationship with? Your people of peace are a great starting place for responding to God's call. Pray for opportunities to share your faith, for the conversations to come up naturally, and for the boldness to respond.

Q. How will you practically engage with God's mission in this world?

WALKING ON

When we began our journey together, we walked ahead of you, inviting you to walk with us. Over time we've walked side by side. Now we stand behind you, with the road ahead of you as you walk on into the new stages of your adventure with God. We can't tell you who to go to and what to do. But we are confident that there is a call to you and a place for you to love and serve the King. There is a role God has for you in the transformation of society in our day. And by His Spirit He will give you all you need as you respond to the Great Commission – on your watch.

Epilogue

No more dreams, no more fantasies.

She didn't need a tiara. She was still the child of the king, safe, secure. Technically maybe it made her a princess, but actually it was the covenant relationship with her father and the call to represent the king that mattered more. Sure, she was beautiful. Her father had told her she was fearfully and wonderfully made and she trusted him now that she had really got to know him. He was far kinder than she thought and much more powerful. She was amazed that in his plans for the kingdom he had responsibilities for her in mind.

There was a life to be lived, and it didn't need to revolve around her. There was more to this ezer *than a crown and a gown.*

She knew that once upon a time she had had different ideas of happily ever afters, of dreams. She smiled, knowing that this was simply part of her journey. When she was a child she thought as any child would, dressing up, playing fantasy games. But her imagination had been illuminated and ignited for something more than ordinary everyday existence.

Still, she'd learned to put childish ways behind her. Granted, some areas were more stubborn than others, but she didn't do it alone. She had good people in her life to grow and learn from – good people to learn and grow with. She didn't need a knight in shining armour (though he was always welcome!). A man who loved and lived for the king would be a suitable match.

Finally she knew that tiaras, jewels and long satin gloves were pointless attire for the tasks that lay ahead. She was called to get her hands dirty in the world around her, to pour her life into other believers, other kingdom operatives. She was called to mobilise others to represent the king in the world around them. She would get the practical aspects of her life in order, because there was work to be done . . .

Enough reflections, enough of getting lost in her thoughts. It was time. The door was already open. She took a deep breath. She stepped into her day, into her life, into her future . . . a woman.

Brilliant books, wonderful websites . . .

Here's a list of some resources that might help you on your journey.

If you want to understand more about your covenant identity

Breen, Mike, *Covenant and Kingdom: The DNA of the Bible*, 3DM Publishing, 2010.

James, Carolyn Custis, *Lost Women of the Bible*, Zondervan, 2005.

Stibbe, Mark, *The Father You've Been Waiting For*, Authentic Media, 2008.

If you're dealing with the broken pieces of your life

The Father's House Trust: www.fathershousetrust.com

Mind and Soul: www.mindandsoul.info/Groups/108634/Mind_and_Soul.aspx

If you want to get some idea for training for transformation

Foster, Richard, *Celebration of Discipline*, Hodder & Stoughton, 1988.

Ortberg, John, *The Life You've Always Wanted*, Zondervan, 2002.

Saxton, Jo, *Real God, Real Life*, Hodder & Stoughton, 2010.

Willard, Dallas, *The Divine Conspiracy*, Fount, 1998.

If you want to invest in your relationships

Abell, Sarah, *Authentic: Relationships from the Inside Out*, Hodder & Stoughton, 2009.

Chapman, Gary, *The Five Love Languages*, Northfield Publishing, 1995.

Cloud, Dr Henry and Townsend, Dr John, *Boundaries in Marriage*, Zondervan, 2002.

Lee, Nicky and Lee, Sila, *The Marriage Book*, Alpha International, 2000.

For a more theological perspective on women, marriage, headship and submission

Bushnell, Katharine, *God's Word to Women*, Christians for Biblical Equality, 2003.

Pierce, Ronald W. and Groothius, Rebecca Merrill, *Discovering Biblical Equality*, IVP Academic, 2004.

Christians for Biblical Equality: www.cbeinternational.org

If you want to learn to disciple others

Breen, Mike and Cockram, Steve, *Building a Discipling Culture*, 3DM Publishing, 2011.

If you want to learn how to handle money better

Credit Action: www.creditaction.org.uk

To change the world on your watch: a few places to start

Tearfund: www.tearfund.org

The Message Trust: www.message.org.uk

XLP (urban youth): www.xlp.org.uk

Compassion: www.compassion.com

International Justice Mission: www.ijm.org

Notes

Prologue

1   Carolyn Custis James, *Half the Church: Recapturing God's Global Vision for Women* (Zondervan, 2011), p. 38.
2   Luke 6:12; cf. Mark 3:14.

Chapter 2

1   Mark Stibbe, *The Father You've Been Waiting For* (Authentic Media, 2005), p. 4.

Chapter 3

1   Clotaire Rapaille, *The Culture Code: An Ingenious Way to Understand Why People Around the World Live and Buy As They Do* (Broadway Books, 2007), p. 58.
2   Sarah Abell, *Authentic Relationships from the Inside Out* (Hodder & Stoughton, 2009), p. 125.
3   Carolyn Custis James, *Half the Church: Recapturing God's Global Vision for Women* (Zondervan, 2011), p. 112.
4   R. David Freeman, 'Woman, a power equal to man', *Biblical Archaeology Review*, vol. 9, 1983, pp. 56–8.

5   Walter Kaiser, 'Correcting caricatures: the biblical teaching on women', *Priscilla Papers*, vol. 19, Spring 2005, pp. 5–11.

6   Carolyn Custis James, *When Life and Beliefs Collide: How Knowing God Makes a Difference* (Zondervan, 2001), p. 187.

7   Michele Guinness, *Woman: The Full Story* (Zondervan, 2003), p. 34.

8   James, *Half the Church*, p. 114.

9   Ibid., p. 112.

10 Guinness, *Woman*, p. 35.

11 Kaiser, 'Correcting caricatures', p. 6.

12 Freeman, 'Woman', pp. 56–8.

13 Carolyn Custis James, *Lost Women of the Bible: The Women We Thought We Knew* (Zondervan, 2005), p. 42.

14 Katharine C. Bushnell, *God's Word to Women* (Christians for Biblical Equality, 2003), pp. 61–3.

15 James, *Lost Women*, p. 42.

16 James, *Half the Church*, p. 114.

Chapter 4

1   Mike Breen, *Covenant and Kingdom: The DNA of the Bible* (3DM Publishing, 2010), p. 29.

2   Ibid.

Chapter 5

1   I've written about spiritual formation – for everyone! – in my book *Real God, Real Life* (Hodder & Stoughton, 2010).

2   John Ortberg, *The Life You've Always Wanted: Spiritual Disciplines for Ordinary People* (Zondervan, 2002), p. 43.

Chapter 6

1 Karen A. Roberto (Director of the Center for Gerontology at Virginia Tech, USA), quoted in Tara Parker-Pope, 'What are friends for? A longer life', *New York Times*, 21 April 2009, p. D1.

2 Mike Breen, *Covenant and Kingdom: The DNA of the Bible* (3DM Publishing, 2010), p. 108.

3 Luke 6:12–16; Mark 3:13–19.

4 John 15:13–15.

5 Ruth 1:20–21.

Chapter 7

1 John 10:10.

2 Genesis 2:18.

3 Taken from our chapter 'Do you fancy a coffee sometime?' from Ali Herbert (comp.), *Worth Knowing: Wisdom for Women* (Survivor, 2007), p. 52.

Chapter 8

1 'The heart matters', interview with Crystal G. Martin in *Oprah* magazine, June 2011, p. 44.

2 Ibid.

3 Check out www.jesuslovesdatemymate.com; it's a fantastic event organised by a church in London, where everyone brings along a friend of the opposite sex who they're not dating but someone else might want to . . .

Chapter 9

1 Tyler Charles, 'True love isn't waiting', *NEUE* magazine, vol. 06, April/May 2011, p. 32.

2 Ibid., p. 35.

Chapter 10

1 Loren Cunningham and David Joel Hamilton, *Why Not Women? A Fresh Look at Scripture on Women in Missions, Ministry and Leadership* (YWAM Publishing, 2001), p. 132.

2 Gordon Fee, 'The cultural context of Ephesians 5:18–6:9', *Priscilla Papers*, vol. 16, no. 1, Winter 2002, p. 6.

3 Dr Gilbert Bilezikan, 'A challenge for proponents of female submission to prove their case from the Bible', Christians for Biblical Equality website at www.cbeinternational.org.

4 A fuller discussion on this is found in Cunningham and Hamilton, *Why Not Women?*, p. 133.

5 Katharine C. Bushnell, *God's Word to Women* (Christians for Biblical Equality, 2003), p. 132.

6 Michele Guinness, *Woman: The Full Story* (Zondervan, 2003), p. 178.

7 Bushnell, *God's Word to Women*, p. 133.

8 Guinness, *Woman*, p. 179.

9 Ibid., p. 34.

10 Ibid., p. 35.

Chapter 12

1 Dr Lois Frankel, *Nice Girls Don't Get the Corner Office* (Hachette, 2010), p. 2.

2 John Ortberg, *The Life You've Always Wanted: Spiritual Disciplines for Ordinary People* (Zondervan, 2002), p. 79.

3 Mike Breen and Steve Cockram, *Building a Discipling Culture* (3DM Publishing, 2009), p. 47.

4 Frankel, *Nice Girls*, p. 201.

5 Ibid., p. 200.

Chapter 13

1   Carolyn Custis James, *Half the Church: Recapturing God's Global Vision for Women* (Zondervan, 2011), p. 192.

2   Peter Greer and Phil Smith, *The Poor Will Be Glad* (Zondervan, 2009), p. 25.

3   Nicholas D. Kristof and Sheryl WuDunn, *Half the Sky: Turning Oppression into Opportunity for Women Worldwide* (Knopf, 2009).

4   Thanks to Peter Greer and the HOPE International team for sharing Chantal's incredible story.

Do you wish this wasn't the end?
Are you hungry for more great teaching, inspiring
testimonies, ideas to challenge your faith?

Join us at www.hodderfaith.com, follow us on Twitter
or find us on Facebook to make sure you get the latest from
your favourite authors.

Including interviews, videos, articles, competitions
and opportunities to tell us just what you thought about
our latest releases.